SpringerBriefs in Applied Sciences and Technology

# PoliMI SpringerBriefs

**Series Editors**
Barbara Pernici, DEIB, Politecnico di Milano, Milano, Italy
Stefano Della Torre, DABC, Politecnico di Milano, Milano, Italy
Bianca M. Colosimo, DMEC, Politecnico di Milano, Milano, Italy
Tiziano Faravelli, DCHEM, Politecnico di Milano, Milano, Italy
Roberto Paolucci, DICA, Politecnico di Milano, Milano, Italy
Silvia Piardi, Design, Politecnico di Milano, Milano, Italy
Gabriele Pasqui, DASTU, Politecnico di Milano, Milano, Italy

Springer, in cooperation with Politecnico di Milano, publishes the PoliMI Springer-Briefs, concise summaries of cutting-edge research and practical applications across a wide spectrum of fields. Featuring compact volumes of 50 to 125 (150 as a maximum) pages, the series covers a range of contents from professional to academic in the following research areas carried out at Politecnico:

- Aerospace Engineering
- Bioengineering
- Electrical Engineering
- Energy and Nuclear Science and Technology
- Environmental and Infrastructure Engineering
- Industrial Chemistry and Chemical Engineering
- Information Technology
- Management, Economics and Industrial Engineering
- Materials Engineering
- Mathematical Models and Methods in Engineering
- Mechanical Engineering
- Structural Seismic and Geotechnical Engineering
- Built Environment and Construction Engineering
- Physics
- Design and Technologies
- Urban Planning, Design, and Policy

http://www.polimi.it

Ilaria Mariani · Marzia Mortati · Francesca Rizzo ·
Alessandro Deserti

# Design Thinking as a Strategic Approach to E-Participation

From Current Barriers to Opportunities

Ilaria Mariani
Department of Design
Politecnico di Milano
Milan, Italy

Marzia Mortati
Department of Design
Politecnico di Milano
Milan, Italy

Francesca Rizzo
Department of Design
Politecnico di Milano
Milan, Italy

Alessandro Deserti
Department of Design
Politecnico di Milano
Milan, Italy

ISSN 2191-530X          ISSN 2191-5318   (electronic)
SpringerBriefs in Applied Sciences and Technology
ISSN 2282-2577           ISSN 2282-2585   (electronic)
PoliMI SpringerBriefs
ISBN 978-3-031-72159-5      ISBN 978-3-031-72160-1   (eBook)
https://doi.org/10.1007/978-3-031-72160-1

Some of the reasoning presented in this work derive from knowledge and insights from the project "AI4GOV, Artificial Intelligence for Public Services", Action No. 2020-EU-IA-0064, co-financed by the EU CEF Telecom (No. INEA/CEF/ICT/A2020/2265375) [ai4gov-hub.eu; ai4gov-master.eu]. The opinions expressed herewith are solely of the authors and do not necessarily reflect the point of view of any EU institution.

© The Editor(s) (if applicable) and The Author(s) 2025. This book is an open access publication.

**Open Access** This book is licensed under the terms of the Creative Commons Attribution 4.0 International License (http://creativecommons.org/licenses/by/4.0/), which permits use, sharing, adaptation, distribution and reproduction in any medium or format, as long as you give appropriate credit to the original author(s) and the source, provide a link to the Creative Commons license and indicate if changes were made.
The images or other third party material in this book are included in the book's Creative Commons license, unless indicated otherwise in a credit line to the material. If material is not included in the book's Creative Commons license and your intended use is not permitted by statutory regulation or exceeds the permitted use, you will need to obtain permission directly from the copyright holder.
The use of general descriptive names, registered names, trademarks, service marks, etc. in this publication does not imply, even in the absence of a specific statement, that such names are exempt from the relevant protective laws and regulations and therefore free for general use.
The publisher, the authors and the editors are safe to assume that the advice and information in this book are believed to be true and accurate at the date of publication. Neither the publisher nor the authors or the editors give a warranty, expressed or implied, with respect to the material contained herein or for any errors or omissions that may have been made. The publisher remains neutral with regard to jurisdictional claims in published maps and institutional affiliations.

This Springer imprint is published by the registered company Springer Nature Switzerland AG
The registered company address is: Gewerbestrasse 11, 6330 Cham, Switzerland

If disposing of this product, please recycle the paper.

# Preface

The potential of technology to enhance public engagement through e-participation and improve the interaction between government and society is nowadays consolidated. However, despite advances, challenges persist in effectively translating citizen input into tangible outcomes. This book specifically explores how Design Thinking (DT) principles and practices can address barriers in e-participation within digital public services, offering a distinct perspective on enhancing citizen engagement. It integrates diverse perspectives from fields such as public policy, information technology, government, and design, providing a holistic understanding of e-participation opportunities for development. Moreover, it provides a comprehensive analysis of current barriers to effective e-participation and infers ways to tackle these barriers grounded in DT methodologies, drawing from various sources including European projects and analysis of literature. Specifically, the analysis presented aligns e-participation barriers with DT principles and practices relevant to overcoming them. It contributes to the ongoing discourse systematising literature at the intersection of multiple fields, to then outline five core DT practices to advance e-participation: (i) Meaning creation and sense-making, (ii) Publics formation, (iii) Co-production, (iv) Experimentation and prototyping, and (v) Changing organisational culture.

The book triangulates qualitative analysis from extensive literature reviews with knowledge from European projects that have experimented with digital tools in public participation. It bridges the theoretical and practical divide, providing rich examples of how digital public services can be significantly enhanced through better public participation. This work stands out by providing a design-driven approach to transforming challenges into opportunities for more effective public engagement, putting the needs of users at the centre.

By combining an academic perspective with operational insights, this book serves as a critical resource for researchers, public employees, civil servants, policymakers, IT and design professionals in the fields of digital transformation and public sector innovation. It equips them with a deeper understanding of the value that DT can bring when working with the public sector with a specific focus on e-participation. In doing this, the book offers a set of strategies and actionable insights for implementing and improving e-participation initiatives. The book's practical orientation is exemplified through the discussion of projects and case studies showcasing the implementation of DT in municipal/governmental e-participation projects, thus outlining successes and lessons learned. The knowledge provided not only illustrates the application of theoretical principles but also offers actionable insights for practitioners.

Milan, Italy
Ilaria Mariani
Marzia Mortati
Francesca Rizzo
Alessandro Deserti

# Acknowledgments

This book is the result of years of research and exploration within the constantly evolving landscape at the crossroad of public engagement, design thinking, and technology, and has been significantly shaped by a long series of European projects and the insights they have provided.

It is with profound gratitude that we acknowledge the support and knowledge contributed by numerous organisations and individuals that have enriched this work. Our deepest thanks go to the teams involved in the European project AI4GOV "Artificial Intelligence for Public Services," co-financed by the EU Connecting Europe Facility. The continuous efforts in exploring how to leverage AI and DT to enhance public services have been instrumental in framing the discussions presented in this book. We also extend our appreciation to the consortia behind the Horizon Europe projects NEUROCLIMA and ORBIS, whose research into AI-based and tech-aided tools for inclusive public participation has broadened our understanding and application of digital technologies in civic engagement. Additional insights were gleaned from other significant European initiatives, including NetZeroCities, SISCODE, and EasyRights, all funded under Horizon 2020, and the GovTech Connect, funded by DG CNECT. These projects provided not only real-world examples but also experiential knowledge, adding a practical perspective that complements the theoretical frameworks presented in the theoretical discourse.

Our gratitude extends to our academic and professional collaborators who have shared their expertise and perspectives with us, enriching the content and depth of our contribution. This publication is greatly related also to our collaborators and co-authors, whose contributions have been essential to both our previous and current projects.

Finally, we are also deeply thankful for the continuous support from our institutional home, the Department of Design of Politecnico di Milano, which has supported not only our researchers but also nurtured a dynamic environment for continuous inquiry and innovation. This nurturing ground has been indeed essential in informing and advancing our research, and outreach activities.

# Contents

1 **Introduction** ............................................. 1
   1.1  Background of This Book ............................. 3
   1.2  Research Methodology ............................... 4
   1.3  Aims and Impact .................................... 6
   References ................................................ 8

2 **The Theoretical Background on E-Participation** .................. 11
   2.1  The Role of Citizens in E-participation: Degrees of Power
        and Influence ..................................... 14
   2.2  Issues and Barriers to Effective E-participation ........... 18
   References ............................................... 25

3 **An Overview on E-Participation** .............................. 31
   3.1  Better Reykjavik: Iceland's Constitutional Reform Process ..... 33
   3.2  VTaiwan .......................................... 35
   3.3  Decidim Barcelona ................................. 38
   3.4  #MyFrance2022 and Make.org ....................... 42
   3.5  CitizenLab for Kapermolen Park ...................... 43
   3.6  Decide Madrid with Consul .......................... 45
   3.7  Scottish's "We Asked, You Said, We Did" .............. 47
   3.8  Open Challenges ................................... 49
   3.9  DT and e-participation .............................. 50
   References ............................................... 51

4 **The Theoretical Background of Design Thinking for Public
   Sector Innovation** ......................................... 57
   4.1  Design Thinking Principles .......................... 58
   4.2  Design Thinking Practices ........................... 60
   References ............................................... 69

| | | | |
|---|---|---|---|
| 5 | **Design Thinking Practices for E-Participation** | | 75 |
| | 5.1 | Meaning Creation and Sense-Making: Valuing the Context and Communicating Better | 75 |
| | | 5.1.1 #MyFrance2022 | 76 |
| | 5.2 | Publics Formation: Engaging Publics Supporting Awareness and Plurality | 77 |
| | | 5.2.1 Better Reykjavik | 78 |
| | | 5.2.2 Decidim Barcelona | 78 |
| | 5.3 | Co-production: From "Asking the Citizens" to "Co-producing with Citizens" | 79 |
| | | 5.3.1 Go Vocal, Former CitizenLab | 80 |
| | 5.4 | Experimenting and Prototyping: Bridging the Gap Between Ideas and Practical Applications | 81 |
| | | 5.4.1 Decide Madrid | 82 |
| | 5.5 | Changing Organisational Culture: Favouring Knowledge Transfer and Capacity Building | 82 |
| | | 5.5.1 vTaiwan | 83 |
| | | 5.5.2 Scottish's "We Asked, You Said, We Did" | 85 |
| | References | | 86 |
| 6 | **Addressing E-Participation Barriers with Design Thinking** | | 89 |
| | 6.1 | E-Participation Barriers Against DT Practices | 89 |
| | 6.2 | A Focus on DT Practices for Public Sector Organisations | 99 |
| | Reference | | 101 |
| 7 | **Future Research Directions** | | 103 |
| | 7.1 | Future DT-Related Research Areas | 103 |
| | | 7.1.1 Assessing DT Effectiveness and Impact on e-participation | 104 |
| | | 7.1.2 Investigating the Impact of DT Implementation in Public Organisations | 104 |
| | | 7.1.3 Tailoring DT Approaches to Context-Specific Barriers and Regulation Frameworks | 105 |
| | | 7.1.4 Exploring Additional DT Methods and Techniques | 106 |
| | 7.2 | Future Research Areas, Beyond DT | 107 |
| | | 7.2.1 Examining Appropriateness of e-participation | 107 |
| | | 7.2.2 Exploring Generative AI Potential | 108 |
| | | 7.2.3 Preventing Biases and the Creation of Echo Chambers | 109 |
| | | 7.2.4 Exploring Asynchronous and Hybrid Interactions | 111 |
| | 7.3 | Limits of the Study | 113 |
| | 7.4 | Conclusions | 113 |
| | References | | 114 |
| **Annex** | | | 117 |

# Chapter 1
# Introduction

**Abstract** This chapter serves as the introduction to this comprehensive study on enhancing e-participation through design thinking (DT) principles. It sets the stage by examining the evolving role of technology in public engagement, the persistent barriers to effective e-participation, and how DT can serve as a transformative tool to overcome these challenges. This chapter outlines the book's scope, establishing the critical importance of integrating DT to foster a more inclusive and effective public discourse. It aims to bridge the theoretical frameworks with practical applications, offering a robust groundwork for the subsequent detailed exploration of DT's application in public sector innovation and citizen engagement.

**Keywords** Context of reference · Methodology · Background · Expected · Audience · Work aim

Scholars have discussed the adoption of technology to strengthen public engagement through e-participation, streamline and enhance the relationship between government and society, and improve accessibility and effectiveness. However, barriers persist, necessitating further research in this area. In such a context, this book explores the pivotal role of design thinking principles and practices within public organisations to overcome the existing barriers in e-participation. Therefore, the book delves into the complex dynamics of e-participation, starting from how it differs from conventional paradigms of citizen engagement and how the evolving role of technology is affecting this landscape. Through a thorough examination of the current state of e-participation, the book goes through the multilayered challenges and limitations of the current e-participation models, shedding light on the transformative potential of DT. It underscores the need for a comprehensive **understanding and critical analysis of contemporary technological and design trends**, advocating for a systemic approach to adequately give citizens a voice and space where to express their views, thereby paving the way for informed decision-making and strategic interventions.

By critically exploring the intersection of technology, design, and governance, the book aims to first provide a literature review at the intersection of e-participation, unravelling the underlying complexities of e-participation practices, and design thinking, to highlight how it can be leveraged to better design citizens participation in the public discourse exploiting technological possibilities for increasing effective engagement. Moreover, by analysing e-participation barriers emerging from the literature and aligning them with notions in the DT literature, this book identifies five core DT practices to enhance e-participation: (i) Meaning creation and sense-making, (ii) Publics formation, (iii) Co-production, (iv) Experimentation and prototyping, and (v) Changing organisational culture. As a result, this book provides insights into enhancing tech-aided public engagement and promoting inclusivity for translating citizen input into tangible service implementations. The book employs a mixed-methods approach, triangulating qualitative analysis of relevant literature in the fields of e-participation and DT, with knowledge from European projects experimenting with public participation activities implying experimentation with digital tools. It foregrounds practical implementation over abstract theorisation, and bridges the academic discourse with real-world applications, offering actionable insights and pragmatic solutions for practitioners and policymakers alike. By doing so, this research aims to bridge the gap between theoretical frameworks and practical application, ultimately contributing to more effective e-participation and digital public services by offering practical insights and actionable strategies for practitioners and policymakers.

Distinctive in its field, the book advocates for a design-driven approach to public participation, highlighting the need to place user needs at the centre of e-participation initiatives as a way to turn challenges into opportunities. By interweaving insights from real-world projects and adopting an interdisciplinary perspective, it provides valuable knowledge applicable across policy-making, information technology, and public sector innovation.

In terms of expected audience, this book is designed to serve as a critical resource for both researchers and practitioners at the intersection of policy, information technology, government, and public engagement. For researchers, it provides a robust analysis of current challenges and opportunities in e-participation, grounding theoretical discussions in practical realities through a comprehensive review of existing practices. This approach not only enriches the academic discourse but also enhances researchers' understanding of how design thinking can be applied effectively for supporting e-participation practices. For practitioners, the book acts as a guide, offering a clear understanding of the possibilities, discussing relevant cases, and presenting actionable insights that help translate theoretical principles into real-world applications. It advances strategies for overcoming barriers to effective e-participation and illustrates how to operationalize design thinking practices to create more inclusive and responsive governance frameworks. By providing concrete examples and case studies, the book serves as a valuable resource for practitioners seeking to operationalise theoretical principles, supporting real implementation of e-participation by tackling issues and barriers to effective e-participation, and offering practical solutions and insights for improvement.

## 1.1 Background of This Book

This book originates from the extensive involvement of the authors in several European projects, particularly those focused on technology for government (GovTech) and the adoption and exploitation of emerging technologies to support governmental operations and activities. Drawing upon a rich body of experience, the book builds upon a comprehensive exploration at the intersection of design, public sector innovation, and technology, with a specific emphasis on e-participation.

The foundational knowledge presented in this book is rooted in a rich scientific discourse spanning multiple fields, mainly including design thinking, public sector innovation, public engagement, and information technology. This interdisciplinary approach not only enriches the theoretical framework but also enhances the practical applicability of the research. The integration of these diverse fields provides a comprehensive lens for dissecting the complexities of e-participation and addressing its multifaceted challenges.

This book benefits from a consistent experimental setting provided by numerous projects funded by the European Commission, as detailed in Annex. These projects have not only provided the authors with first hand knowledge but also offered privileged environments for experimentation, thereby nurturing and validating theoretical insights. Each project contributed distinct perspectives and also empirical data, enabling a comprehensive examination of e-participation through the lens of design as research. This approach, advocated by scholars like Cross (2006), Laurel (2003), and Schön (1983), merges academic inquiry with practical, design-led experimentation, thus bridging the gap between abstract concepts and their real-world applications.

Moreover, the book's methodology is shaped by the research-through-design paradigm (Findeli 1998; Jonas 2007; Koskinen et al. 2011), which encourages the creation of knowledge through making, testing, and reflecting within the context of actual projects. This approach ensures that the theoretical knowledge as well as the practical insights and strategies developed are deeply grounded in reality and directly applicable to improving e-participation frameworks.

By employing this comprehensive and integrative approach, the book aims to uncover the complementary and nuanced perspectives that render e-participation a complex domain requiring an interdisciplinary strategy. As such, it offers a perspective that moves beyond traditional research methods to offer a more dynamic and responsive understanding of how digital platforms can engage citizens and transform public sector operations, easing participation and supporting the shift of its outcomes towards operationalisation.

## 1.2 Research Methodology

The research question to which this book answers is the following: How can the adoption of design thinking principles and practices in public organisations support overcoming some of the current barriers in e-participation?

Through a thorough triangulation of data from diverse sources, including analysis of pertinent literature on e-participation and DT, as well as the analysis of systematic reviews on barriers to e-participation, the book reads and syntheses insights gleaned from European projects, distilling them into a coherent framework that links theoretical insights to practical applications.

Specifically, this book triangulates knowledge from multiple following sources:

- **Analysis of relevant e-participation literature.** The book leverages a review of literature on e-participation spanning from 2000 to 2023, examining both academic and grey literature to ensure a comprehensive understanding of the field. Fundamental publications in the domain are analysed for extracting key concepts, understanding the state-of-the-art, the current topics, and the most relevant challenges.
- **Systematic reviews on e-participation barriers.** For the identification of e-participation barriers, this book builds upon the systematic review conducted by Oliveira and Garcia (2019), which identified a set of barriers to e-participation. The review is conducted with targeted search in major databases, specifically Scopus and IEEE Xplore. This process yields 22 pertinent papers, from which 15 distinct barriers to e-participation are extracted. Our research considers these identified barriers as a baseline to further understand the benefits of DT. Further, this paper is selected as a baseline for barriers because of the citizen-centric perspective that distinguishes it from most of the other systematic reviews on e-participation barriers (i.e., Adnan et al. 2022; Quintero-Angulo et al. 2020; Steinbach et al. 2019), which adopt a public-administration-centric point of view.
- **Analysis of Design Thinking relevant literature.** Having built the landscape on e-participation, the work delved into the literature on DT, selecting contributions that link DT principles and practices to public sector innovation. This involved an analysis of how DT principles can be applied to overcome the identified barriers to e-participation. The work specifically examined the alignment of each e-participation barrier with the relevant DT principles, further highlighting how specific DT activities can help address these challenges.
- **Insights from European projects.** Key insights are drawn from the European project AI4GOV "Artificial Intelligence for Public Services", co-financed by the EU Connecting Europe Facility. Additional knowledge comes from European projects such as the Horizon Europe NEUROCLIMA and ORBIS, which explore AI-based and tech-aided tools for inclusive public participation, and incorporated to enhance the understanding of e-participation and DT. Additional insights come from other European projects experimenting with public participation activities involving digital tools. Specifically, knowledge was derived from the following projects: NetZeroCities (H2020), GovTech Connect (DG CNECT), SISCODE

## 1.2 Research Methodology

(H20202), and EasyRights (H2020). These projects provide real-world examples and experiential knowledge, contributing a practical perspective to complement the theoretical insights from the literature reviews. For further details on each project and their contributions to this work refer to Annex I. Lastly, these projects also contribute 10 experts that are engaged in a validation workshop to provide feedback on the findings presented in this work.

The analysis process was structured into six steps, summarised in Fig. 1.1, and detailed below. Each step builds upon the previous, contributing to a comprehensive approach that intertwines theoretical research with practical application.

1. Below the steps are better detailed:
2. **Analysis of e-participation literature.** Analysis of relevant literature in the e-participation domain, leading to (i) the identification of a set of relevant barriers to e-participation and their characteristics, and (ii) an in-depth understanding of how each barrier hinders e-participation processes.

| | Methodology | Output |
|---|---|---|
| Step 1 **ANALYSIS OF E-PARTICIPATION LITERATURE** | Comprehensive review of literature on e-participation spanning from 2000 to 2023, including both scientific and grey literature. The analysis focuses on extracting key concepts, current trends, and challenges. | Set of relevant barriers to e-participation along with their characteristics, and in-depth understanding of how each barrier affects e-participation processes. |
| Step 2 **ANALYSIS OF DT LITERATURE** | Detailed examination of literature pertaining to DT, focusing on how its principles and practices have been applied in various contexts, particularly in public sector innovation. | Core DT principles and practices significant to e-participation. |
| Step 3 **PRACTICAL KNOWLEDGE INTEGRATION** | Integration of theoretical findings from the e-participation and DT literature reviews with practical insights gained from involvement in several European projects (detailed in Annex I). | Synthesised view combining scholarly insights with real-world experiences, providing a grounded perspective on how to apply DT in e-participation. |
| Step 4 **KNOWLEDGE TRIANGULATION** | Triangulation of data from literature analysis and practical insights to align barriers with corresponding DT practices, evaluating how DT can address specific e-participation challenges. | Coherent framework mapping each identified barrier to specific DT practices, outlining potential interventions for overcoming these barriers. |
| Step 5 **VALIDATION** | Conduction of a validation workshop with 10 experts from the aforementioned projects to gather their expert feedback on the preliminary findings. | Critical insights and perspectives on relevance and feasibility of the findings proposed. |
| Step 6 **REFINEMENT AND REVIEW** | Refinement based on expert feedback and consequent review by the authors. | Finalised study findings that enhance applicability of DT approaches in addressing e-participation barriers. |

**Fig. 1.1** Summary of the research methodology, highlighting steps, methodology, and output for each

3. **Analysis of DT literature.** Analysis of relevant literature on DT to pinpoint core DT principles and significant practices, exploring the application transversal to various contexts, and particularly related to public sector innovation and e-participation, aiming to gain a clear view how DT can support tackling persistent e-participation challenges.
4. **Practical knowledge integration.** Integration of theoretical insights from the literature with practical knowledge acquired through involvement in five European projects—details of these projects are provided in Annex I.
5. **Knowledge triangulation.** Triangulation of theoretical and practical knowledge from the first three steps to align e-participation barriers with DT practices, enabling the identification of (i) how DT can aid in overcoming each barrier, and (ii) specific DT practices that could be employed to mitigate each barrier. The result is a comprehensive understanding that combines scholarly insights with real-world experiences, providing a grounded perspective on applying DT in e-participation.
6. **Validation**. Validation of preliminary findings through a workshop with 10 experts from the five projects listed. Conducted online and facilitated using Miro, the workshop allows experts with extensive experience and complementary expertise in e-participation and DT to provide critical feedback and perspectives which favours grasping the practical relevance and feasibility of the proposed solutions within the framework.
7. **Refinement and review.** Refinement of the preliminary findings based on expert feedback and consequent review by the authors to enhance the work's applicability and relevance. The authors, who have over a decade of experience in both theoretical and applied aspects of public participation and DT, ensured the practicality and relevance of the DT approaches in addressing the barriers to effective e-participation, confirming the validity and applicability of the research's conclusions.

Through this process, each e-participation barrier is linked to a specific DT principle, and practices are provided to illustrate how DT can help enhance e-participation. The triangulation of data from these three distinct sources ensures a multifaceted analysis of how DT can be strategically employed to enhance the effectiveness of e-participation. The book ultimately draws conclusions that contribute to the fields of digital governance and public sector innovation.

## 1.3 Aims and Impact

This book seeks to contribute and further stir the discussion and debate among academics, policymakers, practitioners, and all stakeholders engaged with the challenges and opportunities of e-participation and digital public services. Building on a solid integration of theoretical foundations and practical insights from extensive European projects on the topic of DT principles application for supporting public

## 1.3 Aims and Impact

sector innovation and more inclusive and effective participation of citizens to the public discourse, this work aims to outline a multi-dimensional view on the topic that results into the provision of an integrated design-driven approach and five core DT practices to practically advance e-participation.

To answer such a relevant need emerging from both the theoretical and practical domains, this book spans across fundamental areas of inquiry that shapes the book's structure and content, outlined below:

1. **Systematisation of theoretical and practical knowledge.** Explore how the integration of DT within public organisations can break down existing barriers to e-participation, enhancing the interface between governments and citizens.
2. **Strategic application of DT.** Elaborate on how specific DT practices can be strategically applied to enhance the effectiveness and inclusivity of e-participation initiatives, ensuring that technology truly and more effectively serves the democratic process.
3. **Effective inclusion in the public discourse.** Address how DT can help in making e-participation more accessible and engaging for a broader spectrum of the population, thereby enhancing the democratic discourse.
4. **Operationalisation of theoretical knowledge into practical application.** Provide actionable insights and pragmatic solutions to practitioners aiming to implement e-participation and supporting policies that are both effective and user-centred.
5. **Contribution to Public Sector Innovation.** Frame and discuss the broader implications of adopting DT in public sector innovation, particularly how it can transform the culture within public organisations towards more openness and citizen-centricity.

In light of these areas, the book is structured as follows, offering a comprehensive examination of the evolving landscape of e-participation, DT, and their possible interplay:

- Chapter 1 "Introduction" sets the stage by introducing the work, its motivations, and the structure of the book.
- Chapter 2 "The Theoretical Background on E-Participation" delves into the theoretical aspects, exploring the roles of citizens and identifying the major issues and barriers to effective e-participation.
- Chapter 3 "An Overview of E-Participation" provides a foundational understanding of e-participation practices through relevant case studies.
- Chapter 4 "The Theoretical Background of Design Thinking for Public Sector Innovation" discusses the DT principles and practices as applied to public sector innovation.
- Chapter 5 "Design Thinking Practices for E-Participation" details how DT can enhance e-participation across five key practices: Meaning Creation and Sense-Making; Publics Formation; Co-Production; Experimenting and Prototyping; and Changing Organisational Culture.

- Chapter 6 "Discussion. Enhancing E-Participation through Design Thinking" critically reflects on the implications and significance of the findings of this work.
- Chapter 7 "Future Research Directions" explores potential avenues for future research and summarises the work's outcomes.

Across its chapters, this book leverages case studies and real-world examples to bridge the gap between theoretical insights and practical application, demonstrating how DT can be effectively operationalized within the context of public administration and e-participation. This book aims to equip both scholars and practitioners with a nuanced understanding of how to navigate the complexities of e-participation and foster a more engaged, inclusive, and responsive public sector.

**Funding** Some of the reasoning presented in this work derive from knowledge and insights from the project "AI4GOV, Artificial Intelligence for Public Services", Action No. 2020-EU-IA-0064, co-financed by the EU CEF Telecom (No. INEA/CEF/ICT/A2020/2265375) [ai4gov-hub.eu; ai4gov-master.eu]. The opinions expressed herewith are solely of the authors and do not necessarily reflect the point of view of any EU institution.

# References

Adnan M, Ghazali M, Othman NZS (2022) E-participation within the context of e-government initiatives: a comprehensive systematic review. Telemat Inform Rep 8:100015. https://doi.org/10.1016/j.teler.2022.100015

Cross N (2006) Designerly ways of knowing. Springer, London, UK. https://doi.org/10.1007/1-84628-301-9

Findeli A (1998) A quest for credibility: Doctoral education and research in design at the University of Montreal. Doctoral Education in Design, 1 Jan 1988

Jonas W (2007) Design research and its meaning to the methodological development of the discipline. In: Michel R (ed) Design research now: Essays and selected projects Birkhäuser Basel, Basel, pp 187–206. https://doi.org/10.1007/978-3-7643-8472-2_11

Koskinen I, Zimmerman J, Binder T, Redstrom J, Wensveen S (2011) Design research through practice: from the lab, field, and showroom. Elsevier, Burlington, MA

Laurel B (2003) Design research: methods and perspectives. The MIT Press, Cambridge, MA

Oliveira C, Garcia ACB (2019) Citizens' electronic participation: A systematic review of their challenges and how to overcome them. Int J Web Based Communities 15(2):123–150. https://doi.org/10.1504/IJWBC.2019.101042

Quintero-Angulo RAD, Sánchez-Torres JM, Cardona-Román DM (2020) Problem areas in e-participation: a systematic review. In: Proceedings of the 13th international conference on theory and practice of electronic governance, USA: Association for computing machinery, New York, NY, pp 544–550. https://doi.org/10.1145/3428502.3428584

Schön DA (1983) The reflective practitioner: how professionals think in action. Basic Books, New York, NY

Steinbach M, Sieweke J, Süß S (2019) The diffusion of e-participation in public administrations: a systematic literature review. J Organ Comput Electron Commer 29(2):61–95. https://doi.org/10.1080/10919392.2019.1552749

**Open Access** This chapter is licensed under the terms of the Creative Commons Attribution 4.0 International License (http://creativecommons.org/licenses/by/4.0/), which permits use, sharing, adaptation, distribution and reproduction in any medium or format, as long as you give appropriate credit to the original author(s) and the source, provide a link to the Creative Commons license and indicate if changes were made.

The images or other third party material in this chapter are included in the chapter's Creative Commons license, unless indicated otherwise in a credit line to the material. If material is not included in the chapter's Creative Commons license and your intended use is not permitted by statutory regulation or exceeds the permitted use, you will need to obtain permission directly from the copyright holder.

# Chapter 2
# The Theoretical Background on E-Participation

**Abstract** This chapter explores the theoretical underpinnings of e-participation within e-governance and the critical role of ICTs in facilitating public engagement across governmental levels. It highlights the transformation of e-participation from internal functions to inclusive policy-making processes, supported by ICTs to promote participatory, deliberative, and inclusive democracy. The chapter ultimately goes through the various models and frameworks that describe the spectrum of e-participation, addressing the specific challenges and opportunities that arise in e-governance.

**Keywords** E-participation · E-governance · ICT · Public engagement · Policy-making

E-participation, as conceptualised in the field of e-governance, refers to the integration of ICTs in governmental processes to facilitate public engagement (Macintosh 2004). It concerns technology-mediated interactions of civil society with political or administrative spheres, impacting diverse domains from internal administrative functions to policy-making (Medaglia 2012). Particularly relevant for this work is the definition proposed by the United Nations, which puts citizen engagement at the core of e-participation, relating it less to internal political and administrative procedures and describing it as the process of "engaging citizens through ICTs in policy, decision-making, and service design and delivery so as to make it participatory, inclusive, and deliberative" (United Nations 2018, p. 112). This definition also associates e-participation with providing citizens "with more e-information for decision-making, promoting e-consultation for participation and deliberation processes, and strengthening e-decision-making by improving citizen input" (United Nations 2018, p. 112).

The relevance of e-participation originated from the need to answer the diffused lack of trust in governments caused by the new public management reforms and some political crises that featured the beginning of the twenty-first century (Royo et al. 2023). In response, the paradigm of new public governance (Osborne 2006) emerged, advocating for the active inclusion of citizens, private entities, and varied stakeholders in a networked approach to policy development, implementation, and monitoring (Kann-Rasmussen 2023; Klijn 2008). The effective management of these networks, characterised by cooperation and innovative leadership, is as fundamental as it is challenging (Ansell and Gash 2018; Klijn 2008), suffering from drawbacks such as instability and complex accountability mechanisms (Ansell et al. 2023). For instance, the nature of these networks implies that the more participants are involved, the greater the effort is to ensure that all voices are heard, communications are streamlined and knowledge is shared. Here, e-participation proposes adopting ICTs to better manage these issues and suggests ways to operationalize aspects of e-democracy. Due to these promises, e-participation has garnered considerable attention in the last two decades. Worldwide, governments have adopted e-participation to enhance transparency and citizen involvement in governance (Chun and Cho 2012; Kim and Lee 2012; United Nations 2014, 2022) and service provision (Susha and Grönlund 2012), while scholars and research centres have put forth theories and conceptualisations of the links between e-government and e-participation. In 2016 the OECD (2016) has proposed a pathway to digital government with three main stages: (1) digitisation, where public services are government-centred, and users are passive receivers of government decisions; (2) e-Government, where public services are citizen-centred and users actively participate in service delivery; (3) digital government, where public services are people-driven and users can voice their demands and needs while contributing to forming political priorities. E-participation, as a particular form of public participation, is pivotal in the pathway towards digital government (Fung 2015; Garau 2012; Sieber 2006; Skoric et al. 2016) where both the role of citizens and the channels of interaction with the government are elements in evolution. Under the umbrella of e-government, e-participation aims to ensure that citizens partake in the decision-making process, both to co-decide on policy priorities and to co-produce public services (Panopoulou et al. 2014; Zheng 2017). However, e-participation is more than just effective adoption of technologies. The UN E-Participation Index (EPI)[1] is a recognised benchmark for global e-participation progress that is extensively used for evaluating government efforts in citizen engagement across political systems (Åström et al. 2012; Gulati et al. 2014). Despite its popularity and broad application, the EPI has been recently critiqued for drawing attention on assessing mainly technological aspects (Kabanov 2022) while neglecting the socio-political conditions of the context wherein e-participation occurs (Dilip Potnis and Pardo 2011; Grönlund 2011). This critique opens a discourse on the relevance of looking at e-participation effectiveness beyond its technical achievement, hence making an assessment that is context-aware (Kubicek and Aichholzer 2016).

The progress of e-participation mirrors technological advancements, with its evolution marked by three distinctive generations, paired to some main technology changes that characterised the last two decades. Initially, government-established official spaces for e-participation were prevalent, primarily serving (i) informational and consultative purposes (Medaglia 2012; Panopoulou et al. 2014). The advent of Web 2.0 heralded (ii) a shift towards social media integration, evolving into (iii) the

---

[1] https://publicadministration.un.org/egovkb/en-us/About/Overview/E-Participation-Index.

current landscape that amalgamates advanced technologies for policy input collection from citizens (Charalabidis et al. 2014). However, the literature on the topic points out the predominance of top-down, government-led initiatives of the first kind, facing criticism for limited efficacy and acceptance (Charalabidis et al. 2014; Chun and Cho 2012; Kubicek and Aichholzer 2016; Quittkat 2011).

The academic exploration of e-participation is predominantly forward-looking and with a techno-optimistic vision that focuses on the prospective benefits of digital technology in fostering digital government. Compared with traditional offline participation, e-participation has been regarded as a way to broaden public involvement (Macintosh 2004; Tambouris et al. 2012), enhance trust (Demirdoven et al. 2020; Scherer and Wimmer 2014), legitimise democratic processes (Karlsson 2012; Prosser 2012), and improve policy outcomes (Coelho et al. 2022; Tambouris et al. 2012; Wirtz et al. 2018). Yet, a shift is observable in recent literature, offering a more critical assessment of how e-participation impacts democratic engagement. Recent studies point to the general inefficacy of e-participation initiatives in delivering anticipated results, engaging active users, and including disengaged societal segments (Chun and Cho 2012; Epstein et al. 2014; Karlsson 2012; Kubicek and Aichholzer 2016; Prosser 2012). The challenges in implementing e-participation are often attributed to social, administrative, and institutional factors rather than purely technical ones (Chadwick 2011; Zheng and Zheng 2014).

Research in e-participation commonly explores two consistent themes: (i) identifying barriers and enablers, and (ii) developing strategies for the adoption, implementation, and institutionalisation of e-participation initiatives with a special focus on the diverse roles and degrees of power that citizens can acquire along the spectrum of participation possibilities (Steinbach et al. 2019). Critical views question the effectiveness of citizen engagement in public service design and delivery. This scepticism is attributed to factors such as the perceived lack of citizen knowledge and expertise (Keen 2007 as in Wijnhoven et al. 2015) and concerns about the reduced efficiency in decision-making (Pratt 2005 as in Wijnhoven et al. 2015).

In light of these considerations, a critical understanding of e-participation and its potential enhancement through DT requires a focus on two aspects: first, the role of citizens across the spectrum of power and influence that they acquire through participation; and second, the barriers that impede the achievement of effective e-participation. The forthcoming analysis will delve into these aspects, laying the foundation for examining how DT can be strategically leveraged to bolster e-participation.

## 2.1 The Role of Citizens in E-participation: Degrees of Power and Influence

In the field of e-government, a consistent number of scholars have focused on e-participation, vetting into the role of citizens and describing several types of interactions with the government (Coelho et al. 2022; Rexhepi et al. 2018; Royo et al. 2023; Wijnhoven et al. 2015). These interactions range from citizens as government customers to citizens as partners or co-creators of the public good (Linders 2012). In this wide spectrum of participation, citizens can be engaged in different ways and with different aims. They can be tapped as resources for specific tasks, such as gathering data on particular issues of interest—such as monitoring local traffic patterns and congestion, or identifying areas in need of attention or gathering environmental pollution data—through a process akin to participatory sensing (Ham and Kim 2020). Additionally, citizens can volunteer to participate in public activities, contributing their insights and proposals as subject matter experts. A relevant case in point is civic crowdfunding, where citizens not only suggest initiatives for the public benefit but also potentially finance the most promising ones. When attributed with roles of data gathering, citizens typically assume a more passive position, whereas in proposing ideas, they actively contribute to the generation of innovative and more desirable solutions. By capitalising on these diverse approaches, e-participation opens various opportunities for the public to aid in understanding, conceptualising, or implementing proposals that address societal issues, thereby fostering solutions that are both legitimate and preferable (Simon and Davies 2013). The underlying assumption is that engaging citizens directly in the development and delivery of public services—for instance, in testing and providing feedback on solutions implemented in real-world contexts through small scale experimentations—presents opportunities to assess and improve the effectiveness of public services.

In scholarly discussions, various models of government-citizen interaction have been identified, outlining four established categories (Linders 2012). (i) Citizen Sourcing, where public input informs government decisions; (ii) Government as a platform, emphasising the transfer of knowledge from governments to citizens, aiming at inviting citizens to adopt more sustainable behaviours; (iii) "Do It Yourself" government, characterised by citizen-led initiatives to develop services independently of governmental involvement; and (iv) Collaborative planning and groupware, involving structured dialogues in settings like workshops and training sessions for joint discussion among citizens and government, aimed at facilitating mutual problem-solving. Recent investigations have also proven the value of citizen engagement in administrative tasks to foster greater trust in governmental institutions (Schmidthuber et al. 2019).

## 2.1 The Role of Citizens in E-participation: Degrees of Power and Influence

Several experimentations have been recently conducted, focusing on moving society from a passive to a more active role in the public discourse.[2] These experimentations nurtured several studies and systematic reviews towards the establishment of a common ground and the understanding of the state of the art of how the research addresses e-participation, its gaps and promising directions (Adnan et al. 2022; Santamaría-Philco et al. 2019).

The link between government and citizens can be further framed into various levels of e-participation, considering the varying degrees of power and influence provided to citizens.

Extensive literature exists in the area of public participation providing models which use a single dimension and describe the types of participation possible from lower to higher (Bobbio 2019). Seminal is the ladder of citizen participation of Arnstein (1969) which provided one of the first guides to analyse the degrees of power in public participation and decision making. The ladder presents eight 'rungs' symbolising progressive levels of citizen agency, control and influence in decision-making processes, composing three broad degrees of participation: nonparticipation, where citizens hold no real power; tokenism, offering an illusion of power; and genuine citizen participation, where citizens exercise tangible and meaningful power. Another relevant model is provided by the International Association for Public Participation (IAP2), consisting of a public participation spectrum composed of five steps: Inform, Consult, Involve, Collaborate and Empower. The exploration of e-participation in scholarly literature mirrors the one-dimensional, ladder-like models initially established in participation studies. Over time, these models have been extensively reviewed and synthesised by scholars, offering insights into the multiple hierarchies and distinct characteristics of e-participation. This work particularly draws from the comprehensive reviews by Santamaría-Philco and colleagues (2019) and Bataineh and Abu-Shanab (2016), who analysed and consolidated various significant works in the field. Table 2.1 summarises some of the most relevant models (OECD 2001; Macintosh 2004; Ahmed 2006; Wimmer 2007; Tambouris et al. 2007; Gatautis 2010; Medimorec et al. 2010; Fedotova et al. 2012; UNDESA 2010, 2012; Teran and Drobnjak 2013; Santamaría-Philco et al. 2019), arranging them according to five levels of participation, as the most used scale in the literature.

While some of the models considered date back to the early 2000s, their foundational contributions to defining levels of e-participation remains pertinent. Although developed at a time when e-participation projects were in their nascent stages, they provide a valuable theoretical framework for understanding the spectrum of citizen engagement in digital governance. It is therefore important to distinguish between the theoretical construct of participation levels and the empirical conclusions drawn from early e-participation experiences. While the latter may require reevaluation in

---

[2] Several projects funded by the European Commission have focused on this recently, for instance Co-VAL is a recent Horizon 2020 project that has aimed at exploring the notion of value created in public administration via the participation of citizens & civil servants. Other examples include: UserCentriCities, DECIDO, ACROSS, Gov3.0, Big Policy Canvas, Policy Cloud, AI4PublicPolicy, DUET, IntelComp, INTERLINK, NetZeroCities, E-Sides, AEGIS, Big Data Ocean, Digitranscope, and the Open Governance Research Exchange repository by TheGovLab.

**Table 2.1** E-participation Levels

| | e-participation levels | | | | |
|---|---|---|---|---|---|
| | 1 | 2 | 3 | 4 | 5 |
| Level description | Citizens are informed (through ICT tools) about aspects of the participation initiative | Citizens are consulted, a bidirectional flow of information exist | ICTs provide citizens and governments with the possibility of establishing channels for discussion | Citizens use communication channels (ICT) to make collaborative decision-making | Citizens have dominant authority in decision-making about a particular initiative |
| OECD (2001) | Information | Consultation | | Active participation | |
| Macintosh (2004) | eEnabling | eEngaging | | | eEmpowering |
| Ahmed (2006) | Information | Consultation | | Active participation | |
| Wimmer (2007) | Informing | Consulting | | Collaborating | Empowering |
| Tambouris et al. (2007) | eInform | eConsult | eInvolve | eCollaborate | eEmpower |
| Gatautis (2010) | Informing | Consulting | Involving | Collaborating | Empowering |
| Medimorec et al. (2010) | Information | Consultation | Cooperation | Co-determination | |
| UNDESA (2010, 2012) | e-Information | e-Consultation | | | e-Decision |
| Fedotova et al. (2012) | Informing | Consulting | Involving | Collaborating | Empowering |
| Teran and Drobnjak (2013) | eInforming | eConsulting | eDiscussion | eParticipation | eEmpowerment |
| Santamaría-Philco et al., (2019) | e-Informing | e-Consulting | | e-Collaborating | |

## 2.1 The Role of Citizens in E-participation: Degrees of Power and Influence

light of advancements in digital technologies and shifts in civic engagement patterns, the levels of e-.participation continue to offer a robust and relevant lens for examining the scope and nature of citizen involvement in e-governance, applicable to the current landscape of e-participation possibilities.

The models under review adopt diverse scales to categorise e-participation levels. Table 2.1 aligns the steps of each model's scale with five widely recognised levels of participation. Subsequently, each level is analysed to assess the balance of power and influence between civil society and government. The levels cover a spectrum that begins with fundamental stages of information provision and tokenism (level 1) and progresses to more sophisticated levels where citizens gain substantial decision-making authority (level 5):

- Level 1 refers to informing citizens, engaging them in a limited way. This level cannot be considered participation de facto but a one-way flow of information from the top (e.g., the government) to the bottom (e.g., citizens). Citizens are merely informed about the objectives and operative programs of public institutions.
- Level 2 refers to consultation and introduces a two-way relationship. It allows the collection of citizens' opinions and feedback on specific public initiatives. Governments establish the topics for consultation, formulate the questions, and oversee the procedure. Still, this level guarantees a limited degree of influence of participants in decision-making, as citizens are invited to contribute their opinions on confined topics.
- Level 3 refers to involving and discussing, and recognises a slightly higher level of influence. It entails community-building activities and engages citizens through multiple public discussion formats (e.g., townhalls).
- Level 4 refers to collaboration and participation, and introduces a discrete degree of influence, operatively involving citizens in public initiatives (e.g., in experimentations with living labs) where people can offer innovative ideas and contribute to shaping public services.
- Level 5 refers to the empowerment of citizens who gain power and influence, namely the possibility to define the process of collaboration and steer its evolution in partnership with the government.

In her analysis of public participation dynamics, Nabatchi (2012) articulates a framework relevant to both traditional and e-participation contexts. She enriches the participation discourse by introducing the dimension of communication—one-way, two-way, and deliberative—to the International Association for Public Participation's Spectrum of Public Participation, and aligns this with corresponding levels of public engagement. Figure 2.1 presents an adaptation of Nabatchi's version of the Public Participation Spectrum (2012), which further streamlines and refine the goal of public participation and its promise to the public. This framework delineates a progression from passive participation, characterised by one-way communication in levels 1 and partly 2, to enhanced citizen empowerment through deliberative formats in level 2 (partly) and beyond. For each level of participation, this spectrum makes evident the governmental goal behind the participation and the promise to the public about considering their perspectives in decision-making.

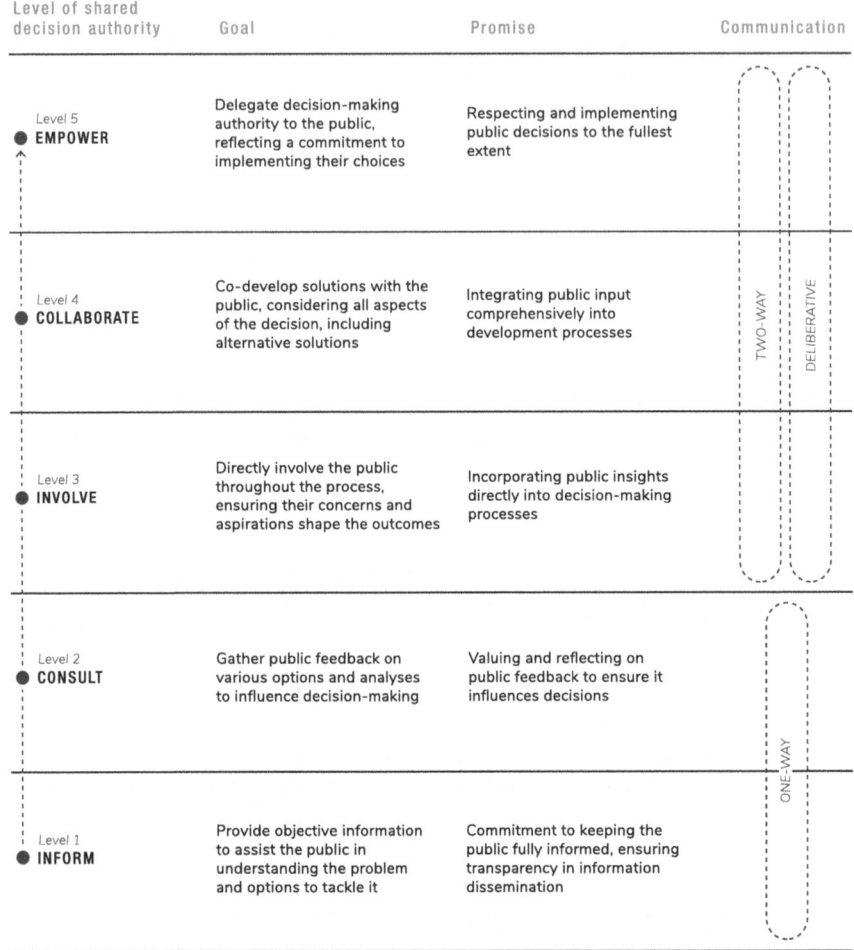

**Fig 2.1.** Adaptation of Nabatchi's version of the Public Participation Spectrum (2012)

## 2.2 Issues and Barriers to Effective E-participation

Current activities in EU member states confirm the will to continue to support and enhance e-participation (Directorate for Communication of the European Committee of the Regions 2019) going beyond mere info-giving and consultations (Recchi 2015) towards proactive engagement. However, despite the relevance of e-participation, the literature discusses several shortcomings, including scattered and heterogeneous knowledge and several common issues and barriers (Quintero-Angulo et al. 2020).

## 2.2 Issues and Barriers to Effective E-participation

The analysis of the literature highlights a multitude of issues, which are summarised in Table 2.2 and analysed below.

**Lack of legitimacy of the approach for policymakers** (Fung 2015). Whether through digital means or traditional methods, consultations with citizens (e.g. through opinion polls) are not seen as a scientifically rigorous method of gauging public opinion, leading to question their credibility and validity in accurately and representatively reflecting public opinions, hence contributing to limiting the impact of such processes on shaping institutional policies and politics (Ganapati and Reddick 2014; Harrison et al. 2011). Although these consultations offer opportunities for diverse voices to be heard and can provide meaningful insights, they may be biased or unrepresentative, depending on their design and communication (Binderkrantz et al. 2021; Røed and Wøien Hansen 2018). Policymakers' reluctance to rely on these methods can significantly limit their impact on shaping policies, as decision-makers may view the inputs as unrepresentative of the broader population or reflecting only

**Table 2.2.** Main issues to achieving effective e-participation and their references to literature

| Issue | Description | Reference |
|---|---|---|
| Lack of legitimacy for policymakers | Citizens' consultations are not seen as rigorous methods for gauging public opinion, leading to questions about their impact on policy | Fung (2015), Ganapati and Reddick (2014), and Harrison et al. (2011) |
| Lack of capacity and need for specialised expertise | New skill sets are required for both civil servants and citizens to effectively implement citizen participation initiatives | Liu (2021), Choi and Song (2020), OECD (2004), and Gupta et al. (2021) |
| Doubts about representativeness, inclusiveness, and equity | Digital platforms may have biases and struggle to balance different democratic models and voices in decision-making | Borge et al. (2022), Kang and Park (2018), and Ruscio (1996) |
| Difficulties in implementing participatory processes | Late stakeholder consultation and unclear pathways to policy outcomes risk making e-participation perceived as tokenistic | Wirtz et al. (2018), Parkinson (2006), OECD (2019), and Galais et al. (2021) |
| Appropriateness of participation in different policy stages | The impact of e-participation varies across policy stages, with significant influence mainly at initial and final stages | Hennen et al. (2020), Steinbach et al. (2019), Michels (2012), and Mintrom and Thomas (2018) |
| Limited focus of tools and methodologies | Tools mainly for interactive communication suggest a gap in early-stage information collection. Varied citizen attitudes towards e-participation tools are influenced by tool design and features | Steinbach et al. (2019), Kopackova et al. (2022), Fischer (2006), Font and Navarro (2013), Sæbø et al. (2011), Mitozo and Marques (2019), Tseng (2023), and Christensen (2021) |

a vocal minority (Fung 2015) depending on how consultations are designed and communicated.

**Lack of capacity and the need for highly specialised expertise** (Liu 2021). The effective implementation of public participation initiatives, such as e-participation, necessitates the development of new skill sets among both civil servants and citizens. Going beyond their traditional administrative roles, civil servants are required to become enablers, facilitators, and collaborators in the participatory process; a condition that implies a change in skills but also a shift in mindset for embracing more open, collaborative approaches to policy-making (Liu 2021). On the other hand, citizens are expected to be actively engaged, contributing meaningful insights and informed discussion. However, a lack of participatory skills can result in lower levels of participation (Choi and Song 2020). Citizens often require training and resources to acquire skills to effectively participate in these processes, especially in contexts where such participation has not been the norm, implying a certain commitment. Pivotal is also the access to technology and information literacy (OECD 2004), since not all citizens may be equally prepared or able to engage in digital platforms for participation (Gupta et al. 2021).

**Doubts about representativeness, inclusiveness, equity, and power balance** (Borge et al. 2022; Kang and Park 2018; Ruscio 1996) continue to be significant challenges in citizen engagement and e-participation. In digital participation platforms, it concerns the potential for demographic biases skewed towards more technologically adept groups (Macintosh 2004). One of the inherent weaknesses of citizen engagement is the difficulty in determining the relative importance of different voices and effectively channelling them into the decision-making process, as well as demonstrating progress and impact. A specific challenge concerns achieving a balance between representative and direct democracy, and between aggregative and deliberative decision-making models (Borge et al. 2022) in a way that genuinely enhances democratic engagement. Furthermore, the lack of diversity and representativeness in e-participation can be exacerbated when processes are not well-designed or when mediated by digital technologies that support the involvement of relatively small and unrepresentative numbers of citizens and focusing on relatively marginal issues.

**Difficulties in implementing participatory processes** as part of the process of policy design (Wirtz et al. 2018). Such challenges are often hindered by a lack of accountability and transparency (Parkinson 2006). Stakeholders are frequently consulted at a late stage, after a policy draft has been developed, limiting the opportunity for their input to be meaningfully integrated into the policy and reducing the overall effectiveness of the participatory process (Chapter 7, OECD 2019). Further, the effectiveness of e-participation is often linked to clarifying how the output of the process influences the democratic process, for instance, leading a change in policy (Galais et al. 2021).[3] Without a clear pathway demonstrating how public input leads

---

[3] This statement draws on a study that examined 70 Advisory Councils. While the study primarily focused on conventional forms of public engagement, its insights about the interdependent relationship between inputs, processes, and outputs, as well as the significance of the concluding evaluation, can be extended to the domain of e-participation as well.

to policy outcomes, e-participation risks being perceived as "democracy-washing". In this case, the participatory process is seen not as a genuine effort to include public input into decision-making, but rather as a tokenistic exercise to legitimise predetermined decisions by public officials. Demonstrating causal relationships and the tangible impact on the participants and the policy-making process can significantly increase the credibility and effectiveness of participatory processes.

**Appropriateness of participation in different policy stages.** The appropriateness of participation in decision-making varies considerably across different areas and stages of the policy process. While e-democracy and e-participation have broadened the scope of public engagement, their influence is mostly observed at the initial and final stages of the policy cycle, with limited impact on the core stages of decision-making and policy execution. Recent studies, such as that of Hennen and colleagues (2020) show that more significant achievements pertain to the enhancement of information access and exchange, rather than direct influence on institutional politics. This observation aligns with what emerges from the analysis of the literature (Steinbach et al. 2019), indicating that current taxonomies of public engagement lack the granularity needed to ascertain the appropriateness of specific types of initiatives (such as citizen juries or user panels) in various social, cultural, and regulatory contexts. This observation confirms established knowledge on how embedding democratic innovations that increase and deepen citizen participation can have varied democratic effects based on their design (Michels 2012). It is then highlighted how the suitability of a specific design depends on the type of policy issue and that tensions between representative and direct democracy are more likely for participatory governance than for deliberative fora (Michels 2012). In this regard, the study of Mintrom and Thomas (2018) highlights the neglected connection between DT and the commissioning of public services. Their study underscores the need for further investigation into how DT can contribute to more effective and appropriate engagement in policy-making.

**Limited focus of applied tools and methodologies to the collection of information** at the beginning of the policy and service design process (ideation) and to the collection of citizens' needs concerning solutions shaped in other contexts (priorities issue). Steinbach and colleagues (2019) highlight the necessity of a broad set of tools for enabling interactive communications, implicitly confirming the absence of consolidated tools and methodologies to support collection of information in the early stages of the process. This issue is reinforced by citizen's mixed attitudes towards existing e-participation tools (Kopackova et al. 2022). While some are motivated to participate in decision-making processes (Fischer 2006), others show diminishing engagement over time (Font and Navarro 2013; Sæbø et al. 2011). This declining participation is further influenced by the design features of the e-participation tools, which can affect citizens' willingness to engage and their perception of the tools' usefulness (Mitozo and Marques 2019; Tseng 2023). These features include, but are not limited to, the ability to interact with politicians and experts, the availability of information, and options for anonymity or identity verification (Christensen 2021).

Ultimately, the persisting challenge of **e-government solutions not adequately meeting user expectations** (Huang and Benyoucef 2014) continues to hinder e-participation (Tavares et al. 2020). Citizen engagement remains a practice needing reinforcement. In response, scholars have highlighted several strategies to mitigate or overcome barriers. Among these proposals, the application of co-creation, DT and co-design methods is emphasised as an approach to include societal contributions early and more consistently throughout the process, thus developing solutions that foster a sense of ownership of public services among citizens (Deserti et al. 2020; European Commission et al. 2020). This work specifically explores ways for integrating DT and co-creation throughout the entire e-participation process. Several studies further discuss this issue, focusing on the barriers to effective e-participation. For instance, the comprehensive systematic literature review conducted by Steinbach and colleagues (2019) thoroughly explores the diffusion of e-participation in public administrations, focusing on stages like adoption, implementation, and institutionalisation across the micro (individuals within an organisation, such as employees and managers), meso (organisation itself, including aspects like its size, culture, and practices), and macro (broader context surrounding the organisation, including elements like national culture, regulations, and societal norms) levels.

Particularly relevant for this work, is the systematic review conducted by Oliveira and Garcia (2019), which identified 15 critical barriers to e-participation, adopting the lens of citizens rather than public administration. These barriers range from digital illiteracy and accessibility challenges to a lack of trust in politicians and a disconnect between public concerns and e-participation topics, as shown in Table 2.3.

The 15 critical barriers identified by Oliveira and Garcia (2019) are very comprehensive of the limits to e-participation including issues like digital illiteracy, which highlights a gap in essential digital skills among citizens, and infrastructural challenges like limited internet access and difficulties due to institutional culture, such as limited capacity to integrate e-participation into government frameworks. Accessibility issues and a general lack of interest in political matters further hinders citizens' interaction with the government. Complexities such as a wide range of political actors and low levels of trust in politicians are also cited as significant hindrances. The authors also highlight issues like unclear language, misalignment of discussed topics with citizens' daily priorities and a general reluctance to contribute feedback. Privacy concerns, unawareness of participation environments, and a paradoxical lack of interest in public affairs despite enthusiasm for new technology are also noted.

Finally, the research highlights issues of transparency and lurking behaviour, where citizens prefer to observe rather than actively participate in e-participation platforms. This compilation of barriers provides a critical understanding of the challenges faced in enhancing citizen engagement in e-governance and underscores the need for targeted strategies to address these multifaceted issues.

The identification of these barriers plays a crucial role in this work, as it lays the foundation for the analysis on how DT can help mitigate them. Understanding the specific obstacles that hinder successful e-participation enables a targeted approach in applying DT principles and practices. This focus on barriers informs the strategic use of DT methodologies, aiming to create more inclusive, accessible, and engaging e-participation practices.

## 2.2 Issues and Barriers to Effective E-participation

**Table 2.3.** Barriers to e-participation joint to degrees of severity (1= easier to solve; 6 = harder to solve) as in Figure 2 and Table 2.2 by Oliveira and Garcia (2019). The column Descriptor is added for better outlining the nature and implications of each barrier in the context of e-participation

| IDs | Barriers | Authors | Descriptor | Degree of severity |
|---|---|---|---|---|
| ID01 | Digital illiteracy | Jung et al. (2015), Sanchez-Nielsen and Lee (2013), Thiel (2016), Charalabidis et al. (2010) | A lack of essential digital skills and competencies among citizens, which hinders their ability to effectively engage in online government platforms | 3 |
| ID02 | Difficult internet access or IT equipment to participate | Thiel (2016) | Limited or no access to the internet and necessary technology, creating a barrier to participate in e-governance | 2 |
| ID03 | Integration of e-participation into the actual government | Sanchez-Nielsen and Lee (2013), Charalabidis et al. (2010) | Challenges in incorporating e-participation tools and processes effectively within existing government structures and workflows | 5 |
| ID04 | Lack of accessibility | Bicking et al. (2011) | Inadequate design and provision of e-government platforms that are not universally accessible to all, including those with disabilities | 1 |
| ID05 | Lack of interest in political issues | Thiel (2016), Sanchez-Nielsen and Lee (2013), Charalabidis et al. (2010), Rexhepi et al. (2016) | A general apathy or disinterest among citizens in political affairs, reducing motivation to participate in e-governance | 5 |
| ID06 | Wide and diverse range of political actors | Sanchez-Nielsen and Lee (2013) | The complexity and variety of political entities and stakeholders involved, which can complicate and hinder effective e-participation | 4 |

(continued)

**Table 2.3.** (continued)

| IDs | Barriers | Authors | Descriptor | Degree of severity |
|---|---|---|---|---|
| ID07 | Low levels of confidence in politicians | Thiel (2016), Sanchez-Nielsen and Lee (2013), Caetano et al. (2017) | A general distrust of politicians and government officials, which discourages active engagement in e-participation initiatives | 6 |
| ID08 | Lack of understanding of the content (unclear language) | Sanchez-Nielsen and Lee (2013), Farina et al. (2013a) | The use of complex or technical language in e-participation platforms that is not easily understood by the general populace | 2 |
| ID09 | Lack of alignment between the topics being discussed and the daily issues and priorities of the citizen | Charalabidis et al. (2010) | The disconnect between the issues addressed in e-participation initiatives and the actual concerns or priorities of everyday citizens | 2 |
| ID10 | Lack of citizens' willingness to produce content, reviews or feedbacks | Charalabidis et al. (2010) | A reluctance or indifference among citizens to actively contribute content, feedback, or reviews on e-participation platforms | 5 |
| ID11 | Privacy issues | Thiel (2016), Sanchez-Nielsen and Lee (2013), Santamaría-Philco et al. (2016) | Concerns over the privacy and security of personal information shared on e-government platforms | 4 |
| ID12 | Unawareness of participation environments | Charalabidis et al. (2010), Bicking et al. (2011) | A lack of awareness or knowledge among the general public about the existence of e-participation opportunities | 3 |

(continued)

**Table 2.3.** (continued)

| IDs | Barriers | Authors | Descriptor | Degree of severity |
|---|---|---|---|---|
| ID13 | Lack of interest in public affairs although enthusiasm for new technology | Thiel (2016) | A paradox where citizens show enthusiasm for new technology but do not translate this interest into engagement in public affairs. | 6 |
| ID14 | Lack of transparency | Potra et al. (2015), Girish et al. (2012), Chaieb et al. (2018), Bolívar (2018a, 2018b) | The perception of insufficient transparency in government operations and decision-making processes, leading to passive online behaviour. | 3 |
| ID15 | Lurking behaviour | Jung et al. (2015) | Citizens' tendency to observe rather than actively participate in e-participation initiatives. | 4 |

**Funding** Some of the reasoning presented in this work derive from knowledge and insights from the project "AI4GOV, Artificial Intelligence for Public Services", Action No. 2020-EU-IA-0064, co-financed by the EU CEF Telecom (No. INEA/CEF/ICT/A2020/2265375) [ai4gov-hub.eu; ai4gov-master.eu]. The opinions expressed herewith are solely of the authors and do not necessarily reflect the point of view of any EU institution.

# References

Adnan M, Ghazali M, Othman NZS (2022) E-participation within the context of e-government initiatives: a comprehensive systematic review. Telemat Inform Rep 8:100015. https://doi.org/10.1016/j.teler.2022.100015l

Ahmed N (2006) An overview of e-participation models. In: UNDESA workshop "e-participation and e-government: Understanding the present and creating the future" Budapest, Hungary, pp 27–28

Ansell C, Gash A (2018) Collaborative platforms as a governance strategy. J Public Adm Res Theory 28(1):16–32. https://doi.org/10.1093/jopart/mux030

Ansell C, Sørensen E, Torfing J (2023) Public administration and politics meet turbulence: the search for robust governance responses. Public Adm 101(1):3–22. https://doi.org/10.1111/padm.12874

Arnstein SR (1969) A ladder of citizen participation. J Am Inst Plann 35(4):216–224. https://doi.org/10.1080/01944366908977225

Åström J, Karlsson M, Linde J, Pirannejad A (2012) Understanding the rise of e-participation in non-democracies: domestic and international factors. Gov Inf Q 29(2):142–150. https://doi.org/10.1016/j.giq.2011.09.008

Bataineh L, Abu-Shanab E (2016) How perceptions of e-participation levels influence the intention to use e-government websites. Transform Gov: People, Process Policy 10(2):315–334. https://doi.org/10.1108/TG-12-2015-0058

Binderkrantz AS, Blom-Hansen J, Senninger R (2021) Countering bias? The EU commission's consultation with interest groups. J Eur Publ Policy 28(4):469–488. https://doi.org/10.1080/13501763.2020.1748095

Bobbio L (2019) Designing effective public participation. Policy Soc 38(1):41–57. https://doi.org/10.1080/14494035.2018.1511193

Borge R, Brugué J, Duenas-Cid D (2022) Technology and democracy: the who and how in decision-making. The cases of Estonia and Catalonia. Profesional de la información [Inf. Prof.] 31(3). https://doi.org/10.3145/epi.2022.may.11

Chadwick A (2011) Explaining the failure of an online citizen engagement initiative: the role of internal institutional variables. J Inform Tech Polit 8(1):21–40. https://doi.org/10.1080/19331681.2010.507999

Charalabidis Y, Loukis EN, Androutsopoulou A, Karkaletsis V, Triantafillou A (2014) Passive crowdsourcing in government using social media. Transform Gov: People, Process Policy 8(2):283–308. https://doi.org/10.1108/TG-09-2013-0035

Choi J-C, Song C (2020) Factors explaining why some citizens engage in e-participation, while others do not. Gov Inf Q 37(4):101524. https://doi.org/10.1016/j.giq.2020.101524

Christensen HS (2021) A conjoint experiment of how design features affect evaluations of participatory platforms. Gov Inf Q 38(1):101538. https://doi.org/10.1016/j.giq.2020.101538

Chun SA, Cho J-S (2012) E-participation and transparent policy decision making. Inf Polity 17(2):129–145. https://doi.org/10.3233/IP-2012-0273

Coelho TR, Pozzebon M, Cunha MA (2022) Citizens influencing public policy-making: resourcing as source of relational power in e-participation platforms. Inf Syst J 32(2):344–376. https://doi.org/10.1111/isj.12359

Demirdoven B, Cubuk EBS, Karkin N (2020) Establishing relational trust in e-participation: a systematic literature review to propose a model. In: Proceedings of the 13th international conference on theory and practice of electronic governance. Association for Computing Machinery, New York, NY, pp 341–348. https://doi.org/10.1145/3428502.3428549

Deserti A, Rizzo F, Smallman M (2020) Experimenting with co-design in STI policy making. Policy Des Pract 3(2):135–149. https://doi.org/10.1080/25741292.2020.1764692

Dilip Potnis D, Pardo TA (2011) Mapping the evolution of e-Readiness assessments. Policy Des Pract 5(4):345–363. https://doi.org/10.1108/17506161111173595

Directorate for communication of the European Committee of the regions (2019) From local to European: putting citizens at the centre of the EU Agenda. EU Commission, Brussels, Belgium. https://www.cor.europa.eu/en/engage/brochures/Documents/From%20local%20to%20European/4082_Citizens%20Consult_brochure_N_FINAL.pdf

Epstein D, Newhart M, Vernon R (2014) Not by technology alone: the "analog" aspects of online public engagement in policymaking. Gov Inf Q 31(2):337–344. https://doi.org/10.1016/j.giq.2014.01.001

European Commission, Directorate-General for Research and Innovation, Iagher R, Monachello R, Warin C, Delaney N, Tornasi Z (2020) Science with and for society in Horizon 2020: Achievements and recommendations for Horizon Europe. Publications Office, Brussels, Belgium. https://doi.org/10.2777/32018

Fedotova O, Teixeira L, Alvelos H (2012). E-participation in Portugal: evaluation of government electronic platforms. In: 4th conference of ENTERprise information systems – aligning technology, organizations and people (CENTERIS 2012), vol 5 pp 152–161. https://doi.org/10.1016/j.protcy.2012.09.017

Fischer F (2006) Participatory governance as deliberative empowerment: the cultural politics of discursive space. Am Rev Public Adm 36(1):19–40. https://doi.org/10.1177/0275074005282582

Font J, Navarro C (2013) Personal experience and the evaluation of participatory instruments in Spanish cities. Public Adm 91(3):616–631. https://doi.org/10.1111/j.1467-9299.2012.02106.x

# References

Fung A (2015) Putting the public back into governance: the challenges of citizen participation and its future. Public Adm Rev 75(4):513–522. https://doi.org/10.1111/puar.12361

Galais C, Fernández-Martínez JL, Font J, Smith G (2021) Testing the input-process-output model of public participation. Eur J Polit Res 60(4):807–828. https://doi.org/10.1111/1475-6765.12427

Ganapati S, Reddick CG (2014) The use of ICT for open government in U. S. municipalities. Public Perform Manag Rev 37(3):365–387. https://doi.org/10.2753/PMR1530-9576370302

Garau C (2012) Citizen participation in public planning: a literature review. Int J Sci 1(12):21–44. https://ideas.repec.org/a/adm/journl/v1y2012i12p21-44.html

Gatautis R (2010) Creating public value through eParticipation: wave project. Econ Manag 15(1):483–490

Grönlund Å (2011). Connecting eGovernment to real government—the failure of the UN eParticipation index. In: Janssen M, Scholl HJ, Wimmer MA, Tan Y (eds), Electronic government. Springer Berlin Heidelberg, Berlin, Heidelberg, pp 26–37.

Gulati GJ "Jeff," Williams CB, Yates DJ (2014) Predictors of on-line services and e-participation: a cross-national comparison. Gov Inf Q 31(4):526–533. https://doi.org/10.1016/j.giq.2014.07.005

Gupta S, Mishra ON, Kumar S (2021) Citizen empowerment and adoption of E-governance services: the role of online citizen skills, awareness, and engagement. Int J Electron GovAnce 13(4):386–407. https://doi.org/10.1504/IJEG.2021.121237

Ham Y, Kim J (2020) Participatory sensing and digital twin city: updating virtual city models for enhanced risk-informed decision-making. J Manag Eng 36(3):04020005. https://doi.org/10.1061/(ASCE)ME.1943-5479.0000748

Harrison TM, Guerrero S, Burke GB, Cook M, Cresswell A, Helbig N et al (2011). Open government and e-government: democratic challenges from a public value perspective. In: Proceedings of the 12th annual international digital government research conference: Digital government innovation in challenging times. Association for Computing Machinery, New York, NY, pp 245–253. https://doi.org/10.1145/2037556.2037597

Hennen L, Van Keulen I, Korthagen I, Aichholzer G, Lindner R, Nielsen, RØ (eds) (2020). European e-democracy in practice. Springer Nature, Cham. https://doi.org/10.1007/978-3-030-27184-8

Huang Z, Benyoucef M (2014) Usability and credibility of e-government websites. Gov Inf Q 31(4):584–595. https://doi.org/10.1016/j.giq.2014.07.002

Kabanov Y (2022) Refining the UN E-participation Index: introducing the deliberative assessment using the varieties of democracy data. Gov Inf Q 39(1):101656. https://doi.org/10.1016/j.giq.2021.101656

Kang HJ, Park EH (2018) Effects of expectation-disconfirmation regarding the role of government on trust in government and the moderating effect of citizen participation. J Policy Stud 3:1–22. https://hdl.handle.net/10371/146811

Kann-Rasmussen N (2023) Reframing instrumentality: from new public management to new public governance. Int J Cult Policy 30(5):583–596. https://doi.org/10.1080/10286632.2023.2239262

Karlsson M (2012) Democratic legitimacy and recruitment strategies in eParticipation projects. In: Charalabidis Y, Koussouris S (eds) Empowering open and collaborative governance: technologies and methods for online citizen engagement in public policy making. Springer, Berlin, Heidelberg, pp 3–20. https://doi.org/10.1007/978-3-642-27219-6_1

Kim S, Lee J (2012) E-participation, transparency, and trust in local government. Public Adm Rev 72(6):819–828. https://doi.org/10.1111/j.1540-6210.2012.02593.x

Klijn E-H (2008) Governance and governance networks in Europe. Public Manag Rev 10(4):505–525. https://doi.org/10.1080/14719030802263954

Kopackova H, Komarkova J, Horak O (2022) Enhancing the diffusion of e-participation tools in smart cities. Cities 125:103640. https://doi.org/10.1016/j.cities.2022.103640

Kubicek H, Aichholzer G (2016) Closing the evaluation gap in e-participation research and practice. In: G Aichholzer, H Kubicek, L Torres (eds) Evaluating e-Participation: frameworks, practice, evidence. Springer, Cham, pp 11–45. https://doi.org/10.1007/978-3-319-25403-6_2

Linders D (2012). From e-government to we-government: defining a typology for citizen coproduction in the age of social media. In: Social media in government - selections from the 12th annual

international conference on digital government research (dg.o2011), 29(4):446–454. https://doi.org/10.1016/j.giq.2012.06.003
Liu HK (2021) Crowdsourcing: citizens as coproducers of public services. Policy Internet 13(2):315–331. https://doi.org/10.1002/poi3.249
Macintosh A (2004) Characterizing e-participation in policy-making. In: Proceedings of the 37th Annual Hawaii international conference on system sciences, 10 pp. https://doi.org/10.1109/HICSS.2004.1265300
Medaglia R (2012) EParticipation research: moving characterization forward (2006–2011). Gov Inf Q 29(3):346–360. https://doi.org/10.1016/j.giq.2012.02.010
Medimorec D, Parycek P, Schossböck J (2010) Vitalizing democracy through e-participation and open government: an Austrian and Eastern European perspective. Bertelsmann Stiftung, p 2020
Michels A (2012) Citizen participation in local policy making: design and democracy. Int J Public Adm 35(4):285–292. https://doi.org/10.1080/01900692.2012.661301
Mintrom M, Thomas M (2018) Improving commissioning through design thinking. Policy Des Pract 1(4):310–322. https://doi.org/10.1080/25741292.2018.1551756
Mitozo I, Marques FPJ (2019) Context matters! Looking beyond platform structure to understand citizen deliberation on Brazil's portal e-Democracia. Policy Internet 11(3):370–390. https://doi.org/10.1002/poi3.196
Nabatchi T (2012) Putting the "public" back in public values research: designing participation to identify and respond to values. Public Adm Rev 72(5):699–708. https://doi.org/10.1111/j.1540-6210.2012.02544.x
OECD (2001) Citizens as partners. Information, consultation and public participation in policy-making. OECD Publishing, Paris. https://doi.org/10.1787/9789264195561-en
OECD (2004) Promise and problems of E-democracy. https://doi.org/10.1787/9789264019492-en
OECD (2016) Digital government strategies for transforming public services in the welfare areas. OECD Publishing, Paris. https://www.oecd.org/gov/digital-government/Digital-Government-Strategies-Welfare-Service.pdf
OECD (2019) Government at a Glance 2019. OECD Publishing, Paris. https://doi.org/10.1787/8ccf5c38-en
Oliveira C, Garcia ACB (2019) Citizens' electronic participation: a systematic review of their challenges and how to overcome them. Int J Web Based Communities 15(2):123–150. https://doi.org/10.1504/IJWBC.2019.101042
Osborne SP (2006) The new public governance? 1. Public Manag Rev 8(3):377–387. https://doi.org/10.1080/14719030600853022
Panopoulou E, Tambouris E, Tarabanis K (2014) Success factors in designing eParticipation initiatives. Inf Organ 24(4):195–213. https://doi.org/10.1016/j.infoandorg.2014.08.001
Parkinson J (2006) Deliberating in the real world: problems of legitimacy in deliberative democracy. Oxford University Press on Demand, Oxford
Prosser A (2012) eParticipation—did we deliver what we promised? In: Kő A, Leitner C, Leitold H, Prosser A (eds) Advancing democracy, government and governance. Springer, Berlin, Heidelberg, pp 10–18
Quintero-Angulo RAD, Sánchez-Torres JM, Cardona-Román DM (2020) Problem areas in e-participation: a systematic review. In: Proceedings of the 13th international conference on theory and practice of electronic governance. Association for Computing Machinery, New York, NY, pp 544–550. https://doi.org/10.1145/3428502.3428584
Quittkat C (2011) The European Commission's online consultations: a success story? JCMS: J Common Mark Stud 49(3):653–674. https://doi.org/10.1111/j.1468-5965.2010.02147.x
Recchi E (2015). A sterile citizenship? Intra-European mobility and political participation. In Recchi E (ed), Mobile Europe: the theory and practice of free movement in the EU. Palgrave Macmillan UK, London, pp 105–122. https://doi.org/10.1057/9781137316028_6
Rexhepi A, Filiposka S, Trajkovik V (2018) Youth e-participation as a pillar of sustainable societies. J Clean Prod 174:114–122. https://doi.org/10.1016/j.jclepro.2017.10.327

# References

Røed M, Wøien Hansen V (2018) Explaining participation bias in the European Commission's online consultations: the struggle for policy gain without too Much Pain. JCMS: J Common Mark Stud 56(6):1446–1461. https://doi.org/10.1111/jcms.12754

Royo S, Bellò B, Torres L, Downe J (2023) The success of e-participation. Learning lessons from decide Madrid and we asked, you said, we did in Scotland. Policy & Internet 16(1). https://doi.org/10.1002/poi3.363

Ruscio KP (1996) Trust, democracy, and public management: a theoretical argument. J Public Adm Res Theory 6(3):461–477. https://doi.org/10.1093/oxfordjournals.jpart.a024321

Sæbø Ø, Flak LS, Sein MK (2011) Understanding the dynamics in e-participation initiatives: looking through the genre and stakeholder lenses. Gov Inf Q 28(3):416–425. https://doi.org/10.1016/j.giq.2010.10.005

Santamaría-Philco A, Canós Cerdá JH, Penadés Gramaje MC (2019) Advances in e-participation: a perspective of last years. IEEE Access 7:155894–155916. https://doi.org/10.1109/ACCESS.2019.2948810

Scherer S Wimmer MA (2014) Trust in e-participation: literature review and emerging research needs. In: Proceedings of the 8th international conference on theory and practice of electronic governance. Association for Computing Machinery, New York, NY, pp 61–70. https://doi.org/10.1145/2691195.2691237

Schmidthuber L, Piller F, Bogers M, Hilgers D (2019) Citizen participation in public administration: investigating open government for social innovation. R&D Manag 49(3):343–355. https://doi.org/10.1111/radm.12365

Sieber R (2006) Public participation geographic information systems: a literature review and framework. Ann Assoc Am Geogr 96(3):491–507. https://doi.org/10.1111/j.1467-8306.2006.00702.x

Simon J, Davies A (2013) People powered social innovation: the need for citizen engagement. Soc Space: 38–43. https://ink.library.smu.edu.sg/lien_research/118/

Skoric MM, Zhu Q, Goh D, Pang N (2016) Social media and citizen engagement: a meta-analytic review. New Media Soc 18(9):1817–1839. https://doi.org/10.1177/1461444815616221

Steinbach M, Sieweke J, Süß S (2019) The diffusion of e-participation in public administrations: a systematic literature review. J Organ Comput Electron Commer 29(2):61–95. https://doi.org/10.1080/10919392.2019.1552749

Susha I, Grönlund Å (2012) EParticipation research: systematizing the field. Gov Inf Q 29(3):373–382. https://doi.org/10.1016/j.giq.2011.11.005

Tambouris E, Liotas N, Tarabanis K (2007) A framework for assessing eParticipation projects and tools. In: 2007 40th Annual Hawaii International Conference on System Sciences (HICSS'07), pp 90–90. https://doi.org/10.1109/HICSS.2007.13

Tambouris E, Macintosh A, Smith S, Panopoulou E, Tarabanis K, Millard J (2012) Understanding eParticipation state of play in Europe. Inf Syst Manag 29(4):321–330. https://doi.org/10.1080/10580530.2012.716994

Tavares AF, Martins J, Lameiras M (2020). Electronic participation in a comparative perspective: Institutional determinants of performance. In: Rodríguez Bolívar MP, Cortés Cediel ME (eds) Digital government and achieving e-public participation: emerging research and opportunities. IGI Global, pp 87–123.

Teran L, Drobnjak A (2013) An evaluation framework for participation: the VAAs case study. Int J HumIties Soc Sci 7(1):77–85. https://doi.org/10.5281/zenodo.1061259

Tseng Y-S (2023) Rethinking gamified democracy as frictional: a comparative examination of the Decide Madrid and vTaiwan platforms. Soc Cult Geogr 24(8):1324–1341. https://doi.org/10.1080/14649365.2022.2055779

UNDESA (2010) UN E-Government Survey 2010. Leveraging e-government at a time of financial and economic crisis. Department of Economic and Social Affairs, United Nations

UNDESA (2012) UN Global E-Government Survey report 2012: E-Government for people. Department of Economic and Social Affairs, United Nations

United Nations (2014) United Nations E-Government Survey 2014: E-Government for the future we want. United Nations Department of Economic and Social Affairs

United Nations (2018) United Nations E-Government Survey 2018: gearing E-Government to support transformation towards sustainable and resilient societies. United Nations, New York, NY https://digitallibrary.un.org/record/3868848

United Nations (2022) E-Government Survey 2022: the future of digital government. United Nations Department of Economic and Social Affairs. https://desapublications.un.org/sites/default/files/publications/2022-09/Web%20version%20E-Government%202022.pdfu

Wijnhoven F, Ehrenhard M, Kuhn J (2015) Open government objectives and participation motivations. Gov Inf Q 32(1):30–42. https://doi.org/10.1016/j.giq.2014.10.002

Wimmer MA (2007). Ontology for an e-participation virtual resource centre. In: Proceedings of the 1st international conference on theory and practice of electronic governance. Association for Computing Machinery, New York, NY, pp 89–98. https://doi.org/10.1145/1328057.1328079

Wirtz BW, Daiser P, Binkowska B (2018) E-participation: a strategic framework. Int J Public Adm 41(1):1–12. https://doi.org/10.1080/01900692.2016.1242620

Zheng Y (2017) Explaining citizens' e-participation usage: functionality of e-participation applications. Adm & Soc 49(3):423–442. https://doi.org/10.1177/0095399715593313

Zheng L, Zheng T (2014) Innovation through social media in the public sector: information and interactions. ICEGOV 2012 Suppl, 31:S106–S117. https://doi.org/10.1016/j.giq.2014.01.011

**Open Access** This chapter is licensed under the terms of the Creative Commons Attribution 4.0 International License (http://creativecommons.org/licenses/by/4.0/), which permits use, sharing, adaptation, distribution and reproduction in any medium or format, as long as you give appropriate credit to the original author(s) and the source, provide a link to the Creative Commons license and indicate if changes were made.

The images or other third party material in this chapter are included in the chapter's Creative Commons license, unless indicated otherwise in a credit line to the material. If material is not included in the chapter's Creative Commons license and your intended use is not permitted by statutory regulation or exceeds the permitted use, you will need to obtain permission directly from the copyright holder.

# Chapter 3
# An Overview on E-Participation

**Abstract** This chapter provides an overview of e-participation, tracing its evolution from early public involvement initiatives to its current integration with digital technologies. It provides examples of implementations and highlights both the potential and challenges of e-participation practices and platforms. The cases are used to discuss the strategic importance of e-participation in enhancing transparency, legitimacy, and trust in public governance, pointing out the role of digital technologies in broadening the scope and depth of public engagement, transforming traditional models and fostering more direct and meaningful interactions between citizens and governments. Ultimately, it explores open challenges in need to be addressed.

**Keywords** Participatory approaches · E-Democracy · ICT · E-Participation challenges · Public engagement

Since the 1960s, governments have recognised public participation as a key strategy to enhance legitimacy, trust, and the transparency of decision-making processes (Lourenço and Costa 2007; Rosenzweigova et al. 2016). This trend intensified in the early 2000s, particularly in Europe, marked by a significant rise in participatory approaches (Zarei and Nik-Bakht 2021), and reflected a broader initiative to engage citizens more actively in decision-making, improving the quality, transparency, and efficacy of policies and public services (United Nations 2014; Directorate for Communication of the European Committee of the Regions 2019). EU Member States have established a robust tradition of dialogue with citizens, thereby strengthening public engagement in democratic processes. The relevance of public engagement has been widely addressed through literature and public debates also considering multiple levels of governance—from the supranational to the national, regional, and local—with the attempt to bring together civil society and institutions as equal partners (von der Leyen 2019, p. 19).

The advance of Information and Communication Technologies (ICTs) has broadened the scope for public participation (Boudjelida et al. 2016; Fietkiewicz et al. 2017). In response to an escalating institutional distrust and public dissatisfaction of citizens with traditional service models, the literature has put increasing emphasis on the notion of e-democracy discussing the need to renew democratic processes using technology to reinforce the public dialogue (Lindner and Aichholzer 2020). Scholars have discussed the adoption of technology to strengthen public engagement, streamline and enhance the relationship between government and society and improve accessibility, effectiveness, and accountability of Government (Haro-de-Rosario et al. 2018; Porumbescu 2016; Wukich 2021). Beyond the digital dissemination of information, scholars have studied the adoption of technology to simplify public services, and to depict the mechanisms to empower citizens to participate in public decision-making, benefiting from increased levels of information, knowledge, communication and interaction (Spirakis et al. 2010).

In this context, e-participation is understood as the enhancement of participatory processes through ICTs, and emerges as a key component for operationalising e-democracy (Adnan et al. 2022; Wirtz et al. 2018). E-participation suggests processes and mechanisms for putting e-democracy in place (Spirakis et al. 2010), pointing out the benefits for both government and citizens in using electronic media to partake in political and governance processes (Macintosh 2008). As such, e-participation is a foundational component of e-democracy, leveraging ICT to ensure that citizens' voices are influential (Adnan et al. 2022). Numerous scholars have analysed the practices through which e-participation can be enacted (Santamaría-Philco et al. 2019). Examples include online public consultations and policy formulation, citizen-led initiatives, and digital platforms serving purposes such as participatory budgeting, crowdsourcing, e-petition, and e-voting. In their comprehensive systematic review on e-participation, Adnan (2022), Ghazali (2022), and Othman (2022) consolidate multiple scholarly contributions, reporting on its being a bridge that links the objectives of e-government with e-democracy principles.

In large-scale e-participation initiatives where participants generate large amounts of data (textual or otherwise), the sheer volume is often overwhelming and too copious for manual analysis. In such scenarios, technology is being increasingly leveraged for efficiently managing, analysing, and deriving insights from this data. E-participation platforms are progressively experimenting with the integration of AI components to streamline the handling of these extensive datasets (Borchers et al. 2024). For example, clustering algorithms are used to group similar ideas or suggestions together, helping to identify common themes or prevalent issues within the discourse. AI-powered summarisation tools can condense lengthy texts into concise summaries that capture essential points, thus speeding up reviewing processes and aiding in presenting key outcomes to both decision-makers and participants. Feedback generators can provide explanations of complex datasets, explain the reasoning behind conclusions drawn from a large volume of inputs, or elucidate the translation of participant inputs into actionable outcomes, maintaining transparency in the process while enabling stakeholders to understand the foundations of data-driven decisions and how participant inputs are being translated into actionable outcomes. Moreover, as participant numbers grow, AI components can enhance scalability and performance, allowing the management of an increased data load by automating parts of the analysis, keeping high responsiveness.

E-participation has been widely adopted in the practice. Public administrations have adopted e-participation to better address challenges of institutional trust and public service dissatisfaction (Kumar et al. 2017; Porumbescu 2016). Websites, digital platforms, and social media have become democratic fora (Shirazi et al. 2010) to link governments, citizens, and diverse societal stakeholders. For instance, numerous public initiatives have been launched to explore innovative digital participatory formats (Escobar and Elstub 2017).

The following section presents case studies that present and discuss the application of e-participation in supporting public sector decision-making and innovation. These examples delve into the successes and challenges encountered, highlighting both the positive impacts and the limitations of e-participation in practical settings.

## 3.1 Better Reykjavik: Iceland's Constitutional Reform Process

Iceland's journey towards constitutional reform has captured global attention as a revolutionary attempt to crowdsource a constitution, which many have praised as a pioneering step in deliberative democracy (Oddsdóttir 2014). This process has been viewed as setting a standard for democratic engagement, although recognising the specificities of the context being quite unique and progressive in respect of the rest of Europe, often obscuring representation issues within the society. Indeed, like its Nordic counterparts, Iceland consistently ranks highly in international indices measuring rights and inclusion, and is often cited as an exemplar of the Nordic model's success in promoting equitable social development (Andersen et al. 2007).

In 2010 Iceland randomly selected 950 citizens to partake in drafting a new constitution (Landemore 2015), representing a statistically valid cross-section of the nation. Convened for a single day in November 2010, the assembly asserted the need for a new constitution and proposed several key elements, including equal voting rights and national ownership of natural resources. The reform process began with a significant public outreach effort using digital media to inform and engage the Icelandic population. In partnership with civil society organisations, the government launched a series of informational campaigns across online platforms, explaining the objectives of the constitutional reform and the relevance of citizen engagement.

Central to the initiative is the use of an online platform where Icelanders could submit proposals, discuss and debate constitutional issues, and vote on the proposals they support. Named Better Reykjavik, this online platform is put in place to support the process, enabling citizens to co-create solutions for city improvements, from budget allocation to public service enhancements. Specifically, the platform allows residents to submit, discuss, and prioritise suggestions, which are then considered by the city council. This process of co-production not only engages citizens directly in municipal governance but also fosters a shared responsibility in urban development. This platform is designed to be user-friendly, accessible to all citizens, and equipped with tools to ensure constructive and moderated discussions. In the process new technologies are experimented with for moderation and process contribution. Among others, artificial intelligence was introduced to select proposals and moderate dialogues between citizens.

Throughout the process, social media also played a crucial role in facilitating broader engagement and discussion. The Constitutional Council uses Twitter, Facebook, and other social media platforms to post updates, spark discussions, and encourage more people to participate directly on the main e-participation site.

To further increase transparency and involvement, many sessions of the Constitutional Council were live-streamed, and interactive webinars were held where citizens could ask questions and provide feedback in real-time. This approach helped to demystify the process of constitutional drafting and ensured that the council's deliberations were open and accessible to all. Feedback gathered through the e-participation platforms further contributed in shaping the draft constitution. Citizens' proposals and comments were reviewed by the Constitutional Council, and many suggestions were incorporated into the draft. This iterative process aimed at making the constitution genuinely reflecting the will of the Icelandic people.

This case illustrates deliberative democracy as central to the process of drafting a new Constitution, guided by a National Assembly composed of randomly selected citizens reflecting the nation's demographics. This assembly's recommendations formed the basis of the constitutional draft, which emphasised direct democratic processes, environmental stewardship, and the equitable use of national resources. The process itself was open to public input through various media, encouraging a broad participation that was seen as instrumental in crafting a constitution that genuinely reflected the people's will.

Despite the inclusive and innovative approach, the e-participation process faced several challenges (O'Farrell 2023). There is indeed a concern about the digital divide potentially excluding less tech-savicious or rural populations (Landemore 2012). Efforts were made to provide alternative means of participation, but the primary engagement remained online. While the platform was open to all, ensuring that all segments of the population were equally represented and that their voices were heard proved challenging.

The deliberative poll in Iceland was conducted according to the model developed by Fishkin (2011, p. 127), which defines diversity based on the representation of principal public viewpoints among the discussion participants. However, framing diversity as an innate cognitive or psychological characteristic wilfully ignores the social power dynamics of decision-making processes, political representation and how the media constructs marginalised communities. An important claim about deliberative polling is that this method can change people's opinions towards consensus and common ground.

The findings from Iceland's deliberative poll were analysed adopting the frameworks of intersectionality (Hill Collins 2017) and superdiversity (Vertovec 2007)—which specifically vets into the increasing complexity within diversity. These perspectives were consistently integrated, illustrating how intersectional inequalities result in the systematic exclusion of minority groups from democratic mechanisms like deliberative polls (Khazaei 2018). This exclusion undermines the authenticity and public endorsement of outcomes derived from such processes, questioning their legitimacy and the validity of their conclusions.

As a consequence, the deliberative poll originally aiming at being a representative mini-public, showed deficits in diversity, highlighting limitations in how e-participation processes can inadvertently marginalise certain groups. The most marginalised residents, particularly migrants and ethnic minorities, remained thus underrepresented, challenging the legitimacy and the inclusiveness of the constitutional process (Khazaei 2018). Theories of intersectionality and superdiversity highlight these gaps, suggesting that the lack of inclusivity in the constitutional process is a product of structural forces that perpetuate exclusion. Despite these challenges, the constitutional reform process in Iceland is a noteworthy example of direct citizen engagement in foundational aspects of governance. While not without its flaws, this crowdsourcing example represents a significant experiment in enhancing democratic engagement and offers lessons for other nations interested in deepening democratic processes through greater citizen involvement.

Iceland's attempt to crowdsource its constitution through e-participation showcases both the potential and limitations of using digital tools for constitutional reforms. While the process is praised for its openness and the extensive use of technology to engage citizens, critical issues related to inclusivity and representation are also highlighted, pointing out the need to address them to fully realise the benefits of e-participation in governance. The lessons learned from Iceland's experience are already widely recognised and inform strategies and practices for integrating technology more effectively and inclusively.

## 3.2 VTaiwan

The vTaiwan initiative (info.vtaiwan.tw) is an open consultation process launched by the Taiwanese government in 2014. Born during a time of significant social movements and calls for democratic reforms, vTaiwan provides a platform for citizens to propose solutions and participate in voting, thereby directly influencing policymaking. This initiative emerged in response to the public's demand for more inclusive governance, highlighted during the Sunflower Movement, where transparency in government agreements with China was a central issue (Fell 2017). In this context, vTaiwan offered a way to resolve standoffs on critical issues through public consensus. Its strength lies in its participatory rulemaking process, supported by digital tools that move away from the echo chambers typically created by social media (Boulianne et al. 2020; Justwan et al. 2018), aiming instead for a more constructive and inclusive form of policy discussion. This is significantly supported by technology, from the use of collaborative text editors for document sharing to online platforms for surveying public opinion. In particular, vTaiwan employs digital platforms to foster inclusive dialogues between citizens and the government, thereby shaping policies that reflect widespread consensus. The process dynamically allows participants to suggest topics, engage in discussions, and help shape national digital legislation, with transitions between stages determined by consensus within the community (Hsiao et al. 2018). The agreement behind is that the government would utilise the feedback collected during the process to inform legislation on digital economy issues. Its operation is managed by three main parties: (i) issue sponsors, like government agencies that propose drafts of laws and regulations; (ii) editors, as individuals from the Science & Technology Law Institute, a government-sponsored non-governmental organisation, who reformat the drafts to facilitate discussion; and (iii) administrators, who are vTaiwan task force from g0v movement (an open source, open government collaboration in Taiwan), responsible for managing the online platform and updating its content. Although vTaiwan is funded by the government, its operation by volunteers lends it a significant degree of legitimacy (GovLab, n.d.).

vTaiwan is structured around a four-stage process: proposal, opinion collection, reflection, and legislation. The process begins with the proposal stage where issues are identified and discussed both online and offline using tools like Discourse for vibrant discussions, sli.do for sharing documents, and Typeform for administering regular questionnaires. This leads to the opinion stage, where platforms like Pol.is, which leverage machine intelligence to scale up deliberative processes (Small et al. 2023), are used to manage and synthesise public opinions, map out areas of consensus and contention among various groups, meanwhile ensuring that all voices can be heard and considered in policy formulation. The use of real-time data collection and analysis tools helps in identifying consensus points among diverse viewpoints, thus enabling more informed decision-making. The reflection stage follows, featuring in-person stakeholder meetings that are live streamed to ensure transparency and broader participation. Finally, the ratification stage sees the formulation of guidelines, policies, or draft bills, which are then sent to the legislature for approval. The entire process is documented on a comprehensive webpage, allowing both the public and government officials to track the progress of issues (GovLab, n.d.).

Over the first five years, the process engaged over 200,000 citizens and led to the creation of 26 pieces of national legislation, demonstrating a significant impact on Taiwan's digital policy landscape. The use of open source tools—like the aforementioned Pol.is, which is freely available and supported by volunteers—keeps the cost of this process low, while ensuring flexibility and wide accessibility. This approach not only fosters a sense of joint ownership between the government and the public, enhancing trust and legitimacy, but also ensures that even complex issues like telemedicine and online alcohol sales are addressed effectively, balancing consensus-building with rapid response when needed.

A key example of vTaiwan's success occurred in late 2015, when it resolved a prolonged impasse regarding the legalisation of online alcohol sales. Initially, discussions between alcohol merchants, e-commerce platforms, and concerned social groups had stalled without yielding substantive regulations. In March 2016, roughly 450 participants on the vTaiwan platform proposed and voted on potential solutions. This process swiftly led to actionable recommendations, including the restriction of online alcohol sales to specific platforms, mandating credit card payments, and requiring pickups at convenience stores to prevent underage purchases (Horton 2018).

## 3.2 VTaiwan

These community-generated solutions were crafted into a draft bill and subsequently presented to the Parliament. vTaiwan's use of the Pol.is platform was instrumental in facilitating interactions among diverse viewpoints, allowing to achieve a significant consensus.

The regulation of Uber showcased another impactful application of vTaiwan's participatory platform. Addressing the challenges posed by UberX, vTaiwan facilitated a four-week public survey that drew over 4000 participants to crowdsource the agenda for a significant open consultation meeting. This process again relied on Pol.is to capture a wide array of public opinions, forming a coherent body of consensus that directly influenced the regulatory approach taken. The feedback collected through this digital deliberation was then integrated in shaping the new regulatory framework for ride-sharing services. Uber responded positively to the outcomes of this process, agreeing to adhere to the consensus developed. In turn, the Taiwanese Government committed to incorporating these items into new regulatory measures. This case exemplifies how vTaiwan leverages digital tools to enhance public engagement in policymaking, ensuring that the regulations enacted are reflective of the public's needs and contribute to more equitable and effective governance.

More recently, in 2023, vTaiwan started a collaboration with Chatham House and the AI Objectives Institute as part of the OpenAI Democratic Inputs to AI project. This initiative aimed to establish guiding principles for artificial intelligence that respect human rights across diverse cultural and legal landscapes. A key aspect of this project is again the use of Pol.is for extensive public deliberation, alongside trials with Large Language Models (LLMs), such as ChatGPT. The process is structured to ensure comprehensive stakeholder engagement, starting with the identification of critical issues and continuing with gathering and synthesising expert knowledge and broad stakeholder engagement through Pol.is. This was followed by AI-driven analysis of the consultation results to identify major consensus points and areas of contention. The subsequent phase involved in-depth, face-to-face consultations to refine these discussions, addressing more complex or contentious issues. Finally, areas of strong consensus were integrated into the primary policy documents, while contentious issues were earmarked for ongoing discussion. This multi-faceted approach aimed to integrate Taiwan's perspectives and needs into the global AI governance framework, ensuring that the development of AI technologies like ChatGPT could benefit from a wide range of insights.

Since its inception, vTaiwan has facilitated discussions on a variety of national issues, with over 80% of these discussions resulting in concrete governmental actions (Hsiao et al. 2018). This success rate underscores the efficacy of open consultation in bridging the gap between citizens and their government, making policy-making more reflective of public needs and aspirations.

Nevertheless, despite its successes, vTaiwan is not exempt from common challenges such as ensuring broad-based participation across diverse demographic groups and dealing with complex policy issues that require nuanced discussions. The initiative leverages a variety of digital tools to gather and synthesise the opinions of Taiwan's citizens on various policy issues. However, the breadth of participation remains a crucial concern, with issues related to representation of diverse demographic groups—not only in terms of age, education, and income but also including less tech-savvy individuals—essential for the legitimacy and effectiveness of the process.

A further significant challenge concerns maintaining independence in topic selection. As a government-funded and institutionalised initiative, vTaiwan often grapples with constraints imposed by governmental authorities concerning the scope of issues it can address. When authorities choose not to engage on particularly sensitive topics, these are excluded from the vTaiwan deliberative process. This limitation restricts the initiative's ability to operate as a fully autonomous platform, potentially hindering its effectiveness in capturing a comprehensive range of public concerns and opinions on more controversial or critical issues.

Another critical challenge for vTaiwan is the nuanced nature of many policy discussions, which can be difficult to fully capture and address through online platforms alone. While digital tools facilitate broad engagement and can efficiently handle large volumes of inputs, the depth and subtlety of some policy debates may be lost without more direct and detailed deliberation. This issue is compounded by the institutional inertia within government structures, which are often unprepared or unwilling to adopt the agile and iterative approaches that vTaiwan's model requires. Traditional bureaucratic processes can be slow to adapt to such innovative consultation methods, leading to resistance within the system (Hsiao et al. 2018).

## 3.3 Decidim Barcelona

Decidim (https://decidim.org) was developed as part of the EU funded D-CENT project (2013–2016), where the city of Barcelona was a pilot together with Madrid, Helsinki and Reykjavik. Decidim was introduced by the Barcellona City Council in 2016 as an online participatory-democracy platform (Aragón et al. 2017) and an open-source initiative that enables various participative processes such as elections, budgeting, and policy development, alongside assemblies and consultations for decision-making and public discourse. The platform has been successfully implemented in Barcelona for several years and has expanded to hundreds of instances across the European Union, transversally to various institutional contexts—from municipalities to regional governments and NGOs. The success of Decidim is often also attributed to its ability to affect institutional culture within local governments that deploy it. It acts as a conduit for knowledge transfer, enabling cities and organisations to learn from each other's experiences through a rich community and network of practice that shares insights, tools, and methodologies.

Nowadays, Decidim has been adopted by over 450 organisations in 30 countries, evidencing its scalability and adaptability. Such widespread adoption worldwide highlights the platform's scalability and effectiveness in encouraging civic participation.

## 3.3 Decidim Barcelona

Decidim, derived from the Catalan phrase meaning "we decide" in Catalan, represents a transformative approach to civic engagement and participatory democracy through digital means (Feenstra et al. 2017). Originating from Spain's vibrant democratic activism, notably influenced by the 15 M/Indignados movement, Decidim is deeply rooted in democratic aspirations and technological innovations aimed at redefining public participation beyond traditional models (Cardullo et al. 2023). Designed and adopted in response to extensive protests by young people calling for greater direct democracy, the platform has enabled the city's inhabitants to actively engage in the formulation, debate, and execution of policies.

Decidim is notable for its high potential for customisation and experimentation, being a Free and Open Source Software (FOSS). The platform continually evolves through incremental innovation and refinement, introducing novelties in controlled environments that are later scaled up across the platform. This method of piloting features in niche settings before broader application ensures that each innovation is thoroughly tested, refined, and validated before going public. The adoption of a flexible architecture enables developers to tailor or modify the standard functionalities, developing custom modules. These modules can be crafted by individual developers or teams and are often developed and sustained by the broader Decidim community, and if vetted and endorsed by the community, they scale up becoming official components of the platform. Built on Ruby on Rails web-app, it allows various entities like local governments, associations, and NGOs to set up participatory processes for strategic planning, elections, and more. Moreover, the same collaboration between tech activists and local councils, especially in Barcelona and Madrid, where it first saw significant implementation, significantly shaped its development. This democratic aspect is further mirrored in its governance. Decidim is governed by a "social contract" that ensures the platform and its code remain opensource (shared on GitHub), transparent, and inclusive (Cardullo et al. 2023). This contract emphasises privacy, equal opportunity, and democratic integrity, ensuring that all participation is traceable and data handling is ethical, reflecting the platform's commitment to democratic values. This approach is recognised for effectively integrating community input into the municipal decision-making framework, enhancing the trustworthiness and legitimacy of municipal decisions by promoting extensive citizen involvement and deliberative processes, significantly bolstering the city's governance processes (Peña-López 2017).

The platform not only hosts digital tools for democratic engagement but also integrates physical meetings, enhancing the interaction between traditional and digital democratic processes. Web technologies are leveraged to enhance transparency in democratic processes and civic engagement at various administrative levels by combining threaded discussions with aligned comments and adopting a user-friendly interface. Its structure comprises various participatory spaces like assemblies, initiatives, and referendums, each designed to cater to different forms of civic engagement. The platform's architecture supports a diverse range of democratic activities, from local participatory budgeting to strategic planning at national levels. It includes multiple components such as proposals, meetings, and surveys that interact within these spaces to facilitate comprehensive participation processes. For instance, when used for participatory budgeting purposes, multiple components from public meetings and surveys to proposal submissions and final voting can be activated to work synergistically. This feature well represents Decidim's capability to adapt dynamically to different participatory needs.

In the specific case of Barcelona, Decidim is recognised as a cornerstone for engaging citizens directly in the governance process. Here, over a two-month period the platform has facilitated a comprehensive participatory process where almost 40 thousand citizens have actively contributed both online and through physical meetings to diverse types of public discussions. The process is meticulously structured to ensure broad-based community involvement around the following phases:

- **Context setting**. The city council starts by outlining key areas and sectors for development, posting over 1300 proposals on *Decidim.barcelona* for public consideration.
- **Public engagement**. Citizens are encouraged to support, debate, and amend these proposals or introduce new ones through the platform. The process is designed to ensure transparency and inclusivity, allowing for an equitable discussion that is not dominated by any single group or interest.
- **Deliberation and decision-making**. Following the public engagement phase, the city council reviews all contributions, considering factors such as the volume of support, the content of discussions, and the outcomes of face-to-face deliberations. Proposals that garner significant community backing are refined and integrated into the final strategic plan.

Decidim can help bridge online and offline participatory channels, creating a dynamic feedback loop between the city's residents and its administrative body. The resulting strategic plan not only reflected the collective will of Barcelona's populace but also set a precedent for other cities aiming to implement similar participatory governance models.

In Helsinki, Decidim has been used to enhance participatory budgeting initiatives, showcasing adaptability across different cultural and administrative contexts. The approach to participatory budgeting via Decidim allows Helsinki to involve the entire community in deciding how a portion of the city budget is spent, spanning from proposing, to discussing, and voting on projects directly affecting their neighbourhoods.

The process unfolds in several phases:

- **Proposal submission**. Residents submit proposals for projects they believe should receive funding, ranging from small-scale local improvements to larger infrastructure projects.
- **Community discussion and refinement**. Proposals are openly discussed on the Decidim platform, where community members can offer feedback, suggest amendments, and rally support for different initiatives.
- **Voting**. After a period of deliberation, residents vote via Decidim the projects they think should be funded, being ensured by the platform features themselves that the entire process is accessible and transparent.

## 3.3 Decidim Barcelona

Helsinki's use of Decidim for participatory budgeting is acknowledged to go beyond democratising the decision-making process, contributing to fostering a greater sense of community through the direct engagement of citizens in allocating municipal resources.

The effectiveness of Decidim is reflected in its widespread adoption and is recognised as highly related to the active, steady involvement of the Metadecidim community in its governance (decidim.org) (Barandiaran et al. 2024). This community plays a crucial role in the platform's continuous development, ensuring that it remains responsive to the needs of its users and adheres to the principles of open and transparent governance. The community recognises itself as an interconnected network, fully embracing the notion of collaborative work (Latour 2005). This network is dedicated to peer production with multifaceted outcomes, ranging from the Decidim software, the community itself, and innovative participatory mechanisms such as new processes and institutions. These outputs manifest the technical, technopolitical, and political dimensions of the project, respectively. The community, which is actively and constantly engaged, functions as a dynamic force aimed at democratising and refining the intersections of politics and technology. This network is as varied and composite as any modern complex system, encompassing a range of elements like executable code spanning hundreds of thousands of lines, numerous workers across various institutions, rich digital content including vast numbers of proposals and discussions, along with educational tools, hacktivists, care-focused initiatives, feminist scholars, servers, developers, and digital infrastructure like code repositories (Barandiaran et al. 2024). It also includes practical tools used in collaborative settings like reconfigurable tables and panels adorned with post-its, and extends to international communication via Telegram groups, along with essential maintenance functions like notification management and spam filtering.

However, despite its successes and widespread use, Decidim faces challenges such as digital literacy, engagement discrepancies, and the integration of diverse demographic groups. A specific challenge is related to the digital divide, which can limit participation among less tech-savvy populations (Barandiaran et al. 2024). However, continuous innovations in platform functionality and governance models aim to address these issues, enhancing user experience and participatory efficacy.

Looking forward, Decidim is poised to expand its impact by exploring new participatory models and enhancing its technological base. The ongoing development driven by global user communities and the Decidim Association aims to keep the platform at the forefront of digital democracy innovations.

Decidim exemplifies a successful integration of technology and democratic principles, offering a scalable model for global adoption. By continuously evolving in response to user feedback and technological advancements, Decidim is recognised as a critical tool for shaping participatory democracy.

## 3.4 #MyFrance2022 and Make.org

My France 2022 represents one of the largest online citizen consultations undertaken by a public media in France, engaging one million French individuals in the lead-up to the presidential elections. This initiative is developed to address the democratic need to integrate citizen voices into the core of political debates during crucial times such as the presidential campaign.

The widespread political mistrust and diminishing electoral participation seen globally prompted the need to explore innovative strategies to engage citizens comprehensively in the democratic process, while recognising that citizens are eager to contribute to democratic life by proposing actionable solutions. To address this challenge, My France 2022 makes use of make.org, a well-known platform within the European Civic Tech landscape, dedicated to involving the broader public—including individuals, organisations, businesses, and civil society groups—in societal enhancement initiatives. This platform supports the conduction of large-scale, independent, and unbiased consultations, engaging up to millions of people in active participation in democratic processes. Participants can submit and vote on proposals in response to open questions, fostering an environment where citizen input is directly solicited and incorporated into actionable strategies for societal development. The platform's design ensures the easy identification of the most popular ideas, facilitating the transition from suggestion to possible directions to consider for implementation. Additionally, make.org is known for prioritising user privacy with transparent algorithms that safeguard personal information.

In view of the 2022 presidential and legislative elections in France, Make.org partnered with France Bleu and France 3—public service media with strong local ties—to help French citizens articulate their priorities for the nation's future. The My France 2022 initiative is launched to combat democratic erosion by empowering citizens ahead of the elections, serving as a platform in which to intervene for influencing their priorities for the country's future and ensure their concerns are central in the public debate and the presidential campaign. Throughout France, citizens were encouraged to articulate their visions for the country's future, contributing to a forward-looking dialogue about national priorities. From September 2021 to March 2022, a significant online consultation posed the question: "What are the priorities for our country tomorrow?", becoming the most extensive online consultation conducted by civil society, amplified through various media outlets. This extensive civic engagement resulted in the compilation of a Citizen's Agenda, highlighting the top priorities according to the French populace. This agenda is then used as a basis for dialogue between the candidates and the public, ensuring that election discussions addressed the real concerns of the electorate. Presidential candidates are then invited to discuss these priorities, promoting a solid dialogue across media platforms jointly provided by Make.org, France Bleu, and France 3.

Such a proactive engagement is a demonstration of how participatory democracy can be embedded within the broader electoral context, setting My France 2022 apart from other initiatives that often fail to engage beyond a narrow group of active citizens. Moreover, by allowing users to propose and vote on solutions, make.org democratises participation and ensures that the aggregation of public opinion is both transparent and actionable. This approach not only captures the public's vision for future societal developments but also protects user data with stringent algorithmic transparency.

The collaboration with France Bleu and France 3 is instrumental to extend the outreach beyond simple proposal submissions to fostering rich dialogues with candidates on radio and TV. This answers a primary challenge that is recognised in ensuring the legitimacy and representativeness of the consultation process. To address demographic disparities, targeted campaigns on social networks were employed to balance participant demographics accurately. The volume of contributions required sophisticated analytical enhancements to effectively categorise and prioritise the public's input, ensuring that the most relevant and consensus-driven ideas were highlighted. This strategy significantly enriched the election coverage, aligning it closely with the electorate's priorities. Make.org spearheaded this initiative, collaborating with prominent public broadcasters to facilitate a broad-based citizen consultation. This partnership aimed to invert the traditional power dynamics of political campaigns by empowering citizens to define the agenda and challenge candidates to address these public priorities. Reflecting on its outreach results, there is strong potential to scale this model of extensive citizen consultation in other electoral contexts, proving adaptability and effectiveness at engaging citizens at a massive scale.

## 3.5 CitizenLab for Kapermolen Park

Kapermolen Park in Hasselt, Belgium, represents an exemplary case of urban renewal facilitated by CitizenLab, now Go Vocal (govocal.com), a digital democracy platform that leverages the power of citizen participation in city planning and decision-making. This case study explores the first use of CitizenLab for empowering local citizens to collaboratively reimagine and reshape their public space, ultimately influencing the redesign of the park set for reconstruction in 2017 (van Aeken 2017).

CitizenLab is a cloud-based platform that enables city governments to engage citizens directly in governance processes through crowdsourcing and co-creation of ideas and feedback, voting for each other's suggestions and prioritising projects in a collaborative environment. The platform facilitates diverse forms of community engagement through an array of interactive tools, including polls, participatory budgets, and idea collection mechanisms. Moreover, it allows project managers to closely monitor project progress and community input, streamlining the decision-making process. With these tools, administrators can collect and analyse ideas and feedback, engage in online discussions, and manage voting to measure community support, all within a single integrated environment.

The city of Hasselt introduces CitizenLab to tackle a challenge common to many cities: engaging a broad section of the population in urban planning processes effectively, answering lackings of traditional methods like public meetings and surveys that often do not capture the diverse opinions and creative ideas of the wider community. CitizenLab is thus put in place to favour a more dynamic and inclusive approach to understand and integrate public preferences in the park's redesign.

In early 2016, the city of Hasselt implemented CitizenLab as a pilot project for steering Kapermolen Park renovation. The platform is adopted for co-creation and crowd-governance, inviting citizens to share their visions for the new park. Features such as polls and analytics tools are adopted to gauge popular opinions and preferences effectively. Moreover, innovative algorithmic models and NLP technology are employed to make the planning process based on data-driven decision-making and be reflective of the community's desires and expectations. Residents can log into the platform from multiple devices, propose their ideas, and interact with others' suggestions. This ease of use and multi-media approach helps overcome barriers to participation, particularly among those who might feel alienated by more formal civic processes.

The input gathered became instrumental in shaping the final design plans for Kapermolen Park, leading the city to identify key themes and priorities among the suggestions, such as the need for more green spaces, child-friendly areas, and sports facilities. Moreover, the platform's backend analytics also provides valuable insights into demographic preferences, helping the city tailor the park to meet the needs of different user groups effectively. Specifically, the platform allows city officials to capture and analyse a wide range of data submitted by citizens during the engagement process. This data includes not just the content of the suggestions and feedback but also demographic information about the participants, such as age, location within the city, and possibly other factors like occupation or interests, depending on what data the platform collects and the users agree to share.

With these analytics, the city can see patterns and trends in the types of improvements different groups desire. For example, young families might prioritise playgrounds and safety features, whereas older residents might prefer more benches and shaded areas. Sports enthusiasts might advocate for more athletic facilities, and pet owners might request areas designated for dogs. Instead of a one-size-fits-all approach, this segmentation of feedback allows city planners to design public spaces that cater to the nuanced needs of its diverse population, accommodating various activities and preferences.

The success of the CitizenLab initiative in Hasselt also set a precedent for other cities considering similar participatory approaches to urban planning. The case of Kapermolen Park illustrates the potential of digital platforms to democratise the planning process, making it more transparent, inclusive, and responsive to citizens' needs. In terms of sharing learning, the platform page features a consistent array of case studies serving not only as testimonials but also as sources of inspiration, along with multiple resources for continuous learning. For instance, there is a set of guides with practical tips and examples to aid the design and execution of community engagement journeys.

According to Sacramento (Sacramento 2023), since its inception as a Belgian startup, CitizenLab has experienced remarkable growth, becoming Go Vocal. Following a successful million-funding round, the company expanded beyond its original base in the Netherlands extending to over 20 countries, with more than 500 local governments using the platform to manage over 15,000 projects that engage over one million community members. CitizenLab was actively present in various global markets, it primarily focused on six key regions: the United States, the United Kingdom, Belgium, the Netherlands, France, and Germany, tailoring its strategies to align with the distinct cultural and economic contexts of these markets. On the contrary, the current strategy of Go Vocal shows a broader reach and thrive to increase the network of governments collaborating with them to bridge the gap with their residents across all policy domains.

## 3.6 Decide Madrid with Consul

This case examines the implementation and impact of the Decide Madrid initiative (decide.madrid.es), which leveraged the Consul platform to promote e-participation in Madrid's civic processes, facilitating a direct and transparent channel for citizens to influence municipal governance.

Decide Madrid was inaugurated in 2015 by the Madrid City Council as part of a broader commitment by the coalition government of Ahora Madrid to enhance democratic engagement (Royo et al. 2020), being strategically implemented to address specific needs in public engagement and decision-making transparency.

The Decide Madrid platform is designed to offer a suite of participatory tools that cater to diverse citizen needs and preferences, being able to host different activities:

- **Debates**. Citizens can initiate and participate in public discussions on various topics via e-forums, fostering a community-oriented approach to public discourse. Debates can also be created by the city council.
- **Proposals**. Citizens can submit proposals for new policies or changes to existing ones, becoming directly involved in the legislative process, so as to make governance more responsive. They can also request complementary materials and supporting documents. Proposals with 1% of support can move to polling and voting.
- **Polls/Voting**. Polling provides a mechanism for gauging public opinion on specific issues, giving the City Council insights into citizens' preferences and priorities. They can be open to all citizens or to specific districts.
- **Participatory budgeting**. Annually, citizens can decide directly on the allocation of a portion of the municipal budget, promoting financial transparency and accountability. Then, the City Council carries out the projects most voted for by citizens starting the following year.
- **Collaborative legislation.** Legislative texts can be shared with the public to receive comments, and are colour-coded according to the sections they address to ease the identification of areas for improvement. Additionally, preliminary debates can be organised before drafting the texts, facilitating more informed and refined legislative development.

- **Processes**. Organisations are supported in the execution of complex participatory processes, such as urban planning, complex regulatory reforms, or multi-stage participation projects.

Each of these functionalities is designed to empower citizens and ensure their voices are considered in administrative processes. Nevertheless, they are also designed to assist organisations in implementing e-participation more effectively, thereby streamlining their operations and enhancing public involvement, promoting transparency in discussions and outcomes, and ultimately facilitating the transition towards implementation.

The technological backbone of Decide Madrid, is Consul, an e-government and e-participation digital platform originally developed for the Madrid City government, which supports modifications and adaptations by other cities worldwide, encouraging continuous improvement and innovation. The technology's adaptability ensures that it can be tailored to meet the specific engagement and regulatory needs of Madrid and beyond, providing a robust framework for scalable and sustainable civic participation. Initially developed for Madrid, the software has significantly broadened its impact, extending its use to more than 120 organisations across over 20 countries. This widespread adoption demonstrates the software adaptability and effectiveness in meeting diverse engagement and regulatory requirements globally. The platform is particularly noted for its user-friendly interface and accessibility, promoting broad participation across diverse demographic groups. The software declares the e-participation of 90 millions of citizens (Consul Project, consulproject.nl). Moreover, Consul is designed for easy customisation, allowing cities and organisations its tailoring to their specific local contexts and governance frameworks. The proven scalability and versatility of Consul not only enhance Madrid's governance but also establish a global standard for civic technology, demonstrating a model of technological diffusion that promotes sustainable and inclusive e-participation worldwide.

Since its launch, Decide Madrid has registered significant user engagement, with hundreds of thousands of registered participants who have collectively proposed numerous initiatives, many of which have been successfully implemented. The platform has notably enhanced the transparency and accountability of the City Council by making decision-making processes visible and traceable (Royo et al. 2020). Additionally, the initiative received international recognition, winning the United Nations Public Service Award in 2018 for promoting democratic and inclusive governance.

Despite its successes, Decide Madrid faces traditional ongoing challenges such as digital literacy, engagement consistency, and the digital divide, which can limit participation among certain demographic groups. To address these issues, the City Council has implemented outreach and education programs, and has worked to ensure the platform is accessible via multiple devices to those with disabilities. Specifically, Decide Madrid has launched various campaigns to educate the public on how to use the platform effectively, generating awareness of their ability to participate in governance through the platform. Empowering information sessions and workshops are held in various neighbourhoods to engage community members directly and demonstrate the functionalities of the platform, explaining how to navigate the platform, initiate debates, propose changes, and participate in polls and budget allocations.

To further enhance e-participation, the platform adopts a multi-device strategy to lessen technological constraints, being designed to be responsive and accessible on various devices, including smartphones, tablets, and desktop computers. In terms of inclusivity, the platform complies with accessibility standards and includes features like screen reader compatibility, options for text enlargement, and high-contrast visual settings, thus being practically usable by people with visual, auditory, or motor impairments. The future of Decide Madrid likely involves further integration of artificial intelligence and machine learning to better analyse citizen feedback and predict future needs, enhancing the responsiveness of the City Council.

Analysis of Decide Madrid reveals several critical success factors, including strong political support, effective stakeholder engagement, and robust ICT infrastructure. The platform's success is partly attributed to its alignment with broader organisational and governmental support, ensuring its integration into the city's governance framework (Royo et al. 2020).

The impact of Decide Madrid on governance is multifaceted. The public can see real-time updates and outcomes of their contributions, fostering trust in the municipal processes. By engaging with the platform, citizens gain a better understanding of governmental functions and budgeting processes. The platform has led to the implementation of citizen-driven initiatives, reflecting a governance structure that is more responsive to public needs and desires.

## 3.7 Scottish's "We Asked, You Said, We Did"

This case explores the "We asked, you said, we did" e-participation initiative implemented by the Scottish Government, as a practice of e-participation for deliberating and shaping policies. This initiative is born in the Scottish Government, which is known for an approach to policy-making—often referred to as the "Scottish Approach"—which emphasises inclusivity, cooperation, and continuous engagement with the public and stakeholders (Cairney et al. 2016). The "We asked, you said, we did" initiative is integrated into this framework, serving as a bridge between the government and the public, ensuring that the voices of citizens are not only heard but also acted upon. This approach aligns with principles advocating for public services to be built around people and communities (Scottish Government 2011).

The initiative leverages e-consultations on various topics to gather public feedback and inform the citizens about the actions taken based on their input, thereby closing the feedback loop while enhancing transparency. It uses the Citizen Space platform, which is recognised to make governmental processes transparent and to track the lifecycle of public feedback from initiation to conclusion. Since its adoption in 2014, and mandatory use across all government consultations from 2016, the platform has facilitated over a hundred consultations annually (Bellò and Downe 2022).

The Citizen Space platform is designed to enhance transparency and accountability, making asking, saying, and doing phases of each public consultation traceable, thus adhering to commitments of transparency and accountability as outlined in Scotland's National Performance Framework and Open Government Partnership Action Plan.

The process consists of three steps which give the name to the initiative.

- **Consultation publication and feedback collection**. The "We asked" is the phase where the government publishes consultations on the platform and sets the agenda, inviting stakeholders and citizens to submit their public input on specific policy areas.
- **Public input**. The "You said" consists in the collection and publication of all responses shaped as opinions and suggestions, made publicly available on the platform. This step ensures transparency, as the public can see not only what issues are being discussed but also the range of perspectives being expressed.
- **Policy formulation and feedback integration**. The "We did" phase concerns the government reviewing all collected feedback and integrating it into the policy-making process. This phase concerns the translation of public sentiment into actionable policy decisions, reporting the outcomes on the platform while detailing how public input influenced the final policy decisions.

The "We asked, you said, we did" practice has been crucial in embedding a culture of consultation within the Scottish Government. It has improved how consultations are conducted by making them more accessible and transparent, thereby increasing public trust and engagement. The platform is used extensively during various stages of the policy cycle, primarily during policy implementation but also in earlier stages like policy analysis and preparation. This wide usage across the policy cycle helps ensure that public feedback is not only gathered but is also considered during the crucial decision-making phases. Each consultation is then accompanied by a detailed report analysing the feedback and the actions taken by policy makers, contributing to maintaining public trust and government accountability for incorporating citizen input into its policies. An example is the e-consultation on the content and timing of the Scottish independence referendum in 2014, which produced a comprehensive report with key findings which shaped the Scottish Government's proposals for the referendum. Another example is the e-consultation on reforming the Gender Recognition Act, which received over 15,000 responses (Bellò and Downe 2022) with inputs for reforming the Act on areas where it previously had not made decisions.

Despite robust mechanisms in place to incorporate public feedback, several challenges persist affecting the integration of these inputs into policy decisions. Firstly, the way consultation questions are framed can significantly influence the nature and utility of the feedback received; questions that are too narrow or leading may limit the scope of responses and not fully capture public sentiment. Additionally, the commitment of policy teams to genuinely integrate diverse viewpoints into the decision-making process varies, which can lead to inconsistencies in how feedback is used across different government departments. Another challenge lies in the government's capacity to engage with complex and sometimes conflicting stakeholder perspectives, which requires analysis and negotiation skills in order to balance and synthesise towards coherent policy. Such challenges draw attention to the need for continuous training, better question design, and stronger commitment to genuine stakeholder engagement for increasing the effectiveness of public consultations.

Moreover, the process's success also depends on the government's capacity to engage with and consider complex and sometimes conflicting stakeholder perspectives. This aspect is also related to disparities in digital access and skills across Scotland, which pose challenges to the inclusivity of the e-consultation process. Indeed, while digital tools facilitate broader and more convenient access for participation without the need for physical presence, they also highlight existing inequalities in digital capabilities. These disparities can prevent certain segments of the population from fully engaging in the consultation process, potentially leading to skewed feedback and outcomes that do not accurately reflect the views of all citizens, thus impacting truly representativeness and equitability of the outcomes. As a consequence, possible improvements concerns increasing the platform's reach and inclusivity, ensuring that a wider demographic can participate and that their feedback is not only gathered but is also impactful.

## 3.8 Open Challenges

Initiatives like Decidim and the platforms adopted in Iceland and Ireland illustrate the growing trend of digital platforms dedicated to enhancing and amplifying citizen participation. However, while the literature that highlights the strategic importance of e-participation is rich (Copus et al. 2017; Directorate for Communication of the European Committee of the Regions 2019; Goodin and Dryzek 2006; OECD 2004; Sæbø et al. 2008; United Nations 2022), it is possible to still identify several challenges and instances in which technology has not fully lived up to its initial promise of providing greater transparency and more informed decision-making. Scholars report on numerous challenges of e-participation that have not been solved, including the lack of public trust in government (Kang and Park 2018; Porumbescu 2016; Reddick and Norris 2013; Royo et al. 2023), the lack of accountability and transparency (Jaeger and Bertot 2010; Panagiotopoulos et al. 2019; Potra et al. 2015; Reggi and Dawes 2016; Susha and Grönlund 2012), and the limited capacity to effectively operationalise e-participation in existing institutional settings (Bekkers et al. 2013; Liu 2021; Quintero-Angulo et al. 2020; Sæbø et al. 2011). Despite the growing adoption of e-participation, its implementation often remains entrenched in traditional service delivery models. Predominantly, these models are provider-centric, characterised by a top-down approach where services are primarily designed and developed by service providers (i.e., public agencies) with minimal input from service end-users. This model often results in solutions that inadequately address the culture, habits, and needs of the public, thus resulting in larger inefficiencies (i.e., a policy programme failing to meet its objectives) despite the prioritisation of the efficiency goals of the provider.

Other streams of research have also studied the consequences of the disconnect between service provider's goals and service user's needs. In service research (Solomon et al. 1985; Surprenant and Solomon 1987), scholars have long advocated for the relevance of customer engagement to make service delivery more effective (Parida et al. 2019; Trischler and Westman Trischler 2022). Notions of the service encounter (McCallum and Harrison 1985; Solomon et al. 1985), the service interaction (Bitner 1992), the service experience (Forlizzi and Ford 2000; Parker and Heapy 2006), and the theoretical framework of the Service-Dominant Logic (Lusch and Vargo 2006; Vargo and Lusch 2004) all report on the centrality of the exchange of value between service provider and user. Studies on co-creation also advocate for the relevance of the active involvement of users and stakeholders to reach consensus and shared results (Bentzen et al. 2020; Jukić et al. 2019).

Rexhepi, Filiposka, and Trajkovik (Rexhepi et al. 2018), propose a multidimensional approach to e-participation, built on four foundational pillars: game-based learning, citizen co-creation, scenario-based simulation modelling, and design thinking (DT) principles. This approach offers an interesting perspective to the present work as it portrays practical ways for engaging users (in this case youth) in public decision-making (in this case sustainable urban planning). Relevantly, the study also suggests the centrality of DT as an approach to enhance e-participation and overcome the disconnect between service provider and service user logics. However, despite the recognition of DT as a relevant methodology to e-participation, a gap exists in scholarly literature regarding its specific benefits. Further, principles and practices that can help public organisations overcome the disconnect between the promises of e-participation and the difficulties of overcoming institutional barriers are missing.

## 3.9 DT and e-participation

Numerous scholars have examined and recognised the relevance of DT as an approach to innovation, both in the private and public sectors (Brown 2008; Gheerawo 2018; Huq and Gilbert 2017; Mahmoud-Jouini et al. 2016; Martin 2009; McGann et al. 2018; Mortati et al. 2023; Rizzo et al. 2017). The approach is recognised for its capacity to extract meaningful insights from direct engagement with citizens thus developing products and services that better respond to their needs (Beckman and Barry 2007). This trait might position DT as a valuable approach for e-participation in practice. However, scant literature has reconnected theories on DT and e-participation to provide a comprehensive account of their links, report on the specific benefits of adopting DT in e-participation, and depict principles and practices that can help e-participation overcome the disconnect between service users' needs and service provider organisational logics.

This book aims at contributing to address this gap and explore how DT can assist the public sector in leveraging e-participation to align citizens' expectations and public services delivery, promoting a governance model that is both inclusive and responsive. Specifically, this work tackles a few main gaps emerged from the literature: the shortage of critical and conceptual analysis on the relevance of DT to improve citizen-government interactions in the e-participation field (Adnan et al. 2022); the lack of methods to address user expectations in the development of e-government solutions that often leads to reduced acceptance (Huang and Benyoucef 2014; Tavares et al. 2020); and the lack of approaches to introduce citizen-centred public innovation (Elsbach and Stigliani 2018; Y. Huang and Hands 2022). The work provides a critical and conceptual analysis on the integration of DT principles and practices (with particular reference to co-creation and co-design) into e-participation frameworks, discussing how this integration can significantly enhance public participation.

**Funding** Some of the reasoning presented in this work derive from knowledge and insights from the project "AI4GOV, Artificial Intelligence for Public Services", Action No. 2020-EU-IA-0064, co-financed by the EU CEF Telecom (No. INEA/CEF/ICT/A2020/2265375) [ai4gov-hub.eu; ai4gov-master.eu]. The opinions expressed herewith are solely of the authors and do not necessarily reflect the point of view of any EU institution.

# References

Adnan M, Ghazali M, Othman NZS (2022) E-participation within the context of e-government initiatives: a comprehensive systematic review. Telemat Inform Rep 8:100015. https://doi.org/10.1016/j.teler.2022.100015

Andersen TM, Holmström B, Honkapohja S, Korkman S, Söderström Hans Tson, Vartiainen J (2007) The nordic model. Embracing globalization and sharing risks. Res Inst Finn Econ. https://ideas.repec.org/b/rif/bbooks/232.html

Aragón P, Kaltenbrunner A, Calleja-López A, Pereira A, Monterde A, Barandiaran XE, Gómez V (2017) Deliberative platform design: the case study of the online discussions in decidim Barcelona. In: Ciampaglia GL, Mashhadi A, Yasseri T (eds) Social informatics. Springer Int Publ, Cham, pp 277–287

Barandiaran XE, Calleja-López A, Monterde A, Romero C (2024) A technopolitical network for participatory democracy: the future of a collective platform. In: Barandiaran XE, Calleja-López A, Monterde A, Romero C (eds) Decidim, a technopolitical network for participatory democracy: philosophy, practice and autonomy of a collective platform in the age of digital intelligence. Springer Nature Switzerland, Cham, pp 119–133. https://doi.org/10.1007/978-3-031-50784-7_5

Beckman SL, Barry M (2007) Innovation as a learning process: embedding design thinking. Calif Manage Rev 50(1):25–56. https://doi.org/10.2307/41166415

Bekkers V, Tummers LG, Voorberg WH (2013) From public innovation to social innovation in the public sector: a literature review of relevant drivers and barriers. Erasmus University Rotterdam, Rotterdam

Bellò B, Downe J (2022) We asked, you said, we did: assessing the drivers and effectiveness of an e-participation practice in Scotland. Edward Elgar Publishing, Cheltenham, UK. https://doi.org/10.4337/9781800374362.00009

Bentzen TØ, Sørensen E, Torfing J (2020) Strengthening public service production, administrative problem solving, and political leadership through co-creation of innovative public value outcomes. Innov J Public Sect Innov J 25(1):1–28

Bitner MJ (1992) Servicescapes: the impact of physical surroundings on customers and employees. J Mark 56(2):57–71. https://doi.org/10.1177/002224299205600205

Borchers M, Cao T-B, Tavanapour N, Bittner EA (2024) Designing AI-based systems to support the analysis of citizens' inputs from e-participation. In: ECIS 2024 Proceedings. https://aisel.aisnet.org/ecis2024/track23_designresearch/track23_designresearch/7

Boudjelida A, Mellouli S, Lee J (2016) Electronic citizens participation: systematic review. In: Proceedings of the 9th international conference on theory and practice of electronic governance. Association for Computing Machinery, New York, NY, pp 31–39. https://doi.org/10.1145/2910019.2910097

Boulianne S, Koc-Michalska K, Bimber B (2020) Right-wing populism, social media and echo chambers in Western democracies. New Media Soc 22(4):683–699. https://doi.org/10.1177/1461444819893983

Brown T (2008) Design thinking. Harv Bus Rev 86(6):84–92

Cairney P, Russell S, St Denny E (2016) The 'Scottish approach' to policy and policymaking: what issues are territorial and what are universal? Policy Polit 44(3):333–350. https://doi.org/10.1332/030557315X14353331264538

Cardullo P, Ribera-Fumaz R, González Gil P (2023) The Decidim'soft infrastructure': democratic platforms and technological autonomy in Barcelona. Comput Cult (9)

Copus C, Roberts M, Wall R (Eds) (2017) Local government in england: centralisation, autonomy and control. Palgrave Macmillan UK, London. https://doi.org/10.1057/978-1-137-26418-3

Directorate for Communication of the European Committee of the Regions (2019) From local to European: putting citizens at the centre of the EU Agenda. EU Commission, Brussels, Belgium. https://www.cor.europa.eu/en/engage/brochures/Documents/From%20local%20to%20European/4082_Citizens%20Consult_brochure_N_FINAL.pdf

Elsbach KD, Stigliani I (2018) Design thinking and organizational culture: a review and framework for future research. J Manag 44(6):2274–2306. https://doi.org/10.1177/0149206317744252

Escobar O, Elstub S (2017) Forms of Mini-Publics: an introduction to deliberative innovations in democratic practice. New Democracy Foundation. https://www.newdemocracy.com.au/research/research-notes/399-forms-of-mini-publics

Feenstra R, Tormey S, Casero-Ripollés A, Keane J (2017) Refiguring democracy: the Spanish political laboratory. Routledge, London, UK. https://doi.org/10.4324/9781315160733

Fell D (2017) Taiwan's social movements under Ma Ying-jeou. Routledge, London, UK

Fietkiewicz KJ, Mainka A, Stock WG (2017) eGovernment in cities of the knowledge society. An empirical investigation of Smart Cities' governmental websites. Open Innov Public Sect 34(1):75–83. https://doi.org/10.1016/j.giq.2016.08.003

Fishkin JS (2011) When the people speak: deliberative democracy and public Consultation. Oxford University Press. https://doi.org/10.1093/acprof:osobl/9780199604432.001.0001

Forlizzi J, Ford S (2000) The building blocks of experience: an early framework for interaction designers. In: Proceedings of the 3rd conference on designing interactive systems: processes, practices, methods, and techniques. Association for Computing Machinery, New York, NY, USA, pp 419–423. https://doi.org/10.1145/347642.347800

Gheerawo R (2018) Design thinking and design doing: describing a process of people-centred innovation. In: Masys AJ (ed) Security by design: innovative perspectives on complex problems. Springer International Publishing, Cham, pp 11–42. https://doi.org/10.1007/978-3-319-78021-4_2

Goodin RE, Dryzek JS (2006) Deliberative impacts: the macro-political uptake of mini-publics. Polit Soc 34(2):219–244. https://doi.org/10.1177/0032329206288152

GovLab (n.d.) vTaiwan using ditial technology to write digital laws (Case Study). GovLab, New York, NY. https://congress.crowd.law/files/vtaiwan-case-study.pdf

Haro-de-Rosario A, Sáez-Martín A, del Carmen Caba-Pérez M (2018) Using social media to enhance citizen engagement with local government: Twitter or Facebook? New Media Soc 20(1):29–49. https://doi.org/10.1177/1461444816645652

Hill Collins P (2017) Intersectionality and epistemic injustice. In: Kidd IJ, Medina J, Pohlhaus G (eds) The Routledge handbook of epistemic injustice. Routledge, pp 1–10. https://doi.org/10.4324/9781315212043-11

# References

Horton C (2018) The simple but ingenious system Taiwan uses to crowdsource its laws vTaiwan is a promising experiment in participatory governance. But politics is blocking it from getting greater traction. MIT Technology Review. https://www.technologyreview.com/2018/08/21/240284/the-simple-but-ingenious-system-taiwan-uses-to-crowdsource-its-laws/

Hsiao Y-T, Lin S-Y, Tang A, Narayanan D, Sarahe C (2018) vTaiwan: an empirical study of open consultation process in Taiwan. SocArXiv 4. https://doi.org/10.31235/osf.io/xyhft

Huang Z, Benyoucef M (2014) Usability and credibility of e-government websites. Gov Inf Q 31(4):584–595. https://doi.org/10.1016/j.giq.2014.07.002

Huang Y, Hands D (2022) Organisational complexity and change by design. In: Huang Y, Hands D (eds) Design thinking for new business contexts: a critical analysis through theory and practice. Springer International Publishing, Cham, pp 53–76. https://doi.org/10.1007/978-3-030-94206-9_4

Huq A, Gilbert D (2017) All the world's a stage: transforming entrepreneurship education through design thinking. Educ+Training 59(2):155–170. https://doi.org/10.1108/ET-12-2015-0111

Jaeger PT, Bertot JC (2010) Designing, implementing, and evaluating user-centered and citizen-centered e-government. Int J Electron Gov Res 6(2):1–17. https://doi.org/10.4018/jegr.2010040101

Jukić T, Pevcin P, Benčina J, Dečman M, Vrbek S (2019) Collaborative innovation in public administration: theoretical background and research trends of co-production and co-creation. Adm Sci 9(4). https://doi.org/10.3390/admsci9040090

Justwan F, Baumgaertner B, Carlisle JE, Clark AK, Clark M (2018) Social media echo chambers and satisfaction with democracy among Democrats and Republicans in the aftermath of the 2016 US elections. J Elections Public Opin Parties 28(4):424–442. https://doi.org/10.1080/17457289.2018.1434784

Kang HJ, Park EH (2018) Effects of expectation-disconfirmation regarding the role of government on trust in government and the moderating effect of citizen participation 3:1–22. https://hdl.handle.net/10371/146811

Khazaei F (2018) Grounds for dialogue: intersectionality and superdiversity. Amsterdam University Press, Tijdschrift voor Genderstudies. https://doi.org/10.5117/TVGN2018.1.KHAZ

Kumar R, Sachan A, Mukherjee A (2017) Qualitative approach to determine user experience of e-government services. Comput Hum Behav 71:299–306. https://doi.org/10.1016/j.chb.2017.02.023

Landemore H (2012) Democratic reason: the mechanisms of collective intelligence in politics. In: Landemore H, Elster J (eds) Collective wisdom: principles and mechanisms. Cambridge University Press, Cambridge, pp 251–289. https://doi.org/10.1017/CBO9780511846427.012

Landemore H (2015) Inclusive constitution-making: the icelandic experiment. J Polit Philos 23(2):166–191. https://doi.org/10.1111/jopp.12032

Latour B (2005) Reassembling the social: an introduction to actor-network-theory. Oxford University Press, Oxford, UK

Lindner R, Aichholzer G (2020) E-Democracy: conceptual foundations and recent trends. In: Hennen L, van Keulen I, Korthagen I, Aichholzer G, Lindner R, ØR Nielsen (eds) European E-Democracy in practice. Springer International, Cham, Switzerland, pp 11–45. https://doi.org/10.1007/978-3-030-27184-8_2

Liu HK (2021) Crowdsourcing: citizens as coproducers of public services. Policy Internet 13(2):315–331. https://doi.org/10.1002/poi3.249

Lourenço RP, Costa JP (2007) Incorporating citizens' views in local policy decision making processes. Spec Issue Clust 43(4):1499–1511. https://doi.org/10.1016/j.dss.2006.06.004

Lusch RF, Vargo SL (2006) Service-dominant logic: reactions, reflections and refinements. Mark Theory 6(3):281–288. https://doi.org/10.1177/1470593106066781

Macintosh A (2008). E-Democracy and E-Participation research in Europe. In: Chen H, Brandt L, Gregg V, Traunmüller R, Dawes S, Hovy E et al (eds) Digital government: E-Government research, case studies, and implementation. Springer US, Boston, MA, pp 85–102. https://doi.org/10.1007/978-0-387-71611-4_5

Mahmoud-Jouini SB, Midler C, Silberzahn P (2016) Contributions of design thinking to project management in an innovation context. Proj Manag J 47(2):144–156. https://doi.org/10.1002/pmj.21577

Martin RL (2009) The design of business: why design thinking is the next competitive advantage. Harvard Business Press, Cambridge, MA

McCallum JR, Harrison W (1985) Interdependence in the service encounter. The service encounter: Managing employee/customer interaction in service businesses 18(4):35–48

McGann M, Blomkamp E, Lewis JM (2018) The rise of public sector innovation labs: experiments in design thinking for policy. Policy Sci 51(3):249–267. https://doi.org/10.1007/s11077-018-9315-7

Mortati M, Mariani, I, Rizzo F (2023) How design thinking can support the establishment of an EU GovTech ecosystem. In: De Sainz Molestina D, Galluzzo L, Rizzo F, Spallazzo D (eds) IASDR 2023: Life-Changing Design. DRS, Italy, pp 1–29. Presented at the IASDR 2023: Life-Changing Design, Milano. https://doi.org/10.21606/iasdr.2023.356

Oddsdóttir K (2014) Iceland: the birth of the world's first crowd-sourced constitution? Cambridge Int Law J 3(4):1207–1220. https://doi.org/10.7574/cjicl.03.04.246

OECD (2004) Promise and problems of E-Democracy. https://doi.org/10.1787/9789264019492-en

O'Farrell L (2023) Progressive borealism and the diversity deficit in Iceland's constitutional reform process. Social Identities 29(5):462–479. https://doi.org/10.1080/13504630.2024.2324282

Panagiotopoulos P, Edelmann N, Glassey O, Misuraca G, Parycek P, Lampoltshammer T, Re B (2019) Electronic participation. Springer

Parida V, Sjödin D, Reim W (2019) Reviewing literature on digitalization, business model innovation, and sustainable industry: past achievements and future promises. Sustainability 11(2). https://doi.org/10.3390/su11020391

Parker S, Heapy J (2006) The journey to the interface. Demos London, UK.

Peña-López I (2017) decidim.barcelona, Spain. Voice or chatter? Case studies. IT For Change, Bengaluru. http://ictlogy.net/articles/20171010_ismael_pena-lopez_-_dedicim.barcelona_spain_voice_chatter_case_study.pdf

Porumbescu GA (2016) Linking public sector social media and e-government website use to trust in government. Gov Inf Q 33(2):291–304. https://doi.org/10.1016/j.giq.2016.04.006

Potra S, Branea A-M, Izvercian M (2015, January) How to foster prosumption for value co-creation? The open government development plan. Presented at the proceedings of the European Conference on E-Government, ECEG, pp 239–245. https://www.scopus.com/inward/record.uri?eid=2-s2.0-84940825765&partnerID=40&md5=e6a19699688a89435d4eeb42f89ad45f

Quintero-Angulo RAD, Sánchez-Torres JM, Cardona-Román DM (2020). Problem areas in e-participation: a systematic review. In: Proceedings of the 13th international conference on theory and practice of electronic governance. Association for Computing Machinery, New York, NY, USA, pp 544–550. https://doi.org/10.1145/3428502.3428584

Reddick CG, Norris DF (2013) E-participation in local governments: an examination of political-managerial support and impacts. Transform GovMent People Process Policy 7(4):453–476. https://doi.org/10.1108/TG-02-2013-0008

Reggi L, Dawes S (2016) Open government data ecosystems: linking transparency for innovation with transparency for participation and accountability. In: Scholl HJ, Glassey O, Janssen M, Klievink B, Lindgren I, Parycek P et al (eds) Electronic Government. Springer Int Publ, Cham, pp 74–86

Rexhepi A, Filiposka S, Trajkovik V (2018) Youth e-participation as a pillar of sustainable societies. J Clean Prod 174:114–122. https://doi.org/10.1016/j.jclepro.2017.10.327

Rizzo F, Deserti A, Cobanli O (2017) Introducing design thinking in social innovation and in public sector: a design-based learning framework. Eur Public Soc Innov Rev 2(1):127–143

Rosenzweigova I, Skoric V, Asipovich H (2016). Civil participation in decision-making processes: an overview of standards and practices in Council of Europe Member States. https://rm.coe.int/civil-participation-in-decision-making-processes-an-overview-of-standa/1680701801

Royo S, Pina V, Garcia-Rayado J (2020) Decide madrid: a critical analysis of an award-winning e-Participation initiative. Sustainability 12(4). https://doi.org/10.3390/su12041674

Royo S, Bellò B, Torres L, Downe J (2023) The success of e-participation. Learning lessons from decide madrid and we asked, you said, we did in Scotland. Policy & Internet n/a(n/a). https://doi.org/10.1002/poi3.363

Sacramento IB (2023) Branding in the era of artificial intelligence (AI): an examination of hybrid human-AI approach in the rebranding of citizenLab (PhD Thesis). Retrieved from http://hdl.handle.net/10400.26/48569

Sæbø Ø, Rose J, Skiftenes Flak L (2008) The shape of eParticipation: characterizing an emerging research area. Gov Inf Q 25(3):400–428. https://doi.org/10.1016/j.giq.2007.04.007

Sæbø Ø, Flak LS, Sein MK (2011) Understanding the dynamics in e-Participation initiatives: looking through the genre and stakeholder lenses. Gov Inf Q 28(3):416–425. https://doi.org/10.1016/j.giq.2010.10.005

Santamaría-Philco A, Canós Cerdá JH, Penadés Gramaje MC (2019) Advances in e-Participation: a perspective of Last Years. IEEE Access 7:155894–155916. https://doi.org/10.1109/ACCESS.2019.2948810

Scottish Government (2011) Christie commission on the future delivery of public services. https://www.gov.scot/publications/commission-future-delivery-public-services/

Shirazi F, Ngwenyama O, Morawczynski O (2010) ICT expansion and the digital divide in democratic freedoms: an analysis of the impact of ICT expansion, education and ICT filtering on democracy. Telematics Inform 27(1):21–31. https://doi.org/10.1016/j.tele.2009.05.001

Small CT, Vendrov I, Durmus E, Homaei H, Barry E, Cornebise J et al (2023) Opportunities and risks of LLMs for scalable deliberation with Polis. https://arxiv.org/abs/2306.11932

Solomon MR, Surprenant C, Czepiel JA, Gutman EG (1985) A role theory perspective on dyadic interactions: the service encounter. J Mark 49(1):99–111. https://doi.org/10.1177/002224298504900110

Spirakis G, Spiraki C, Nikolopoulos K (2010) The impact of electronic government on democracy: e-democracy through e-participation. Electron GovMent Int J 7(1):75–88. https://doi.org/10.1504/EG.2010.029892

Surprenant CF, Solomon MR (1987) Predictability and personalization in the service encounter. J Mark 51(2):86–96. https://doi.org/10.1177/002224298705100207

Susha I, Grönlund Å (2012) EParticipation research: systematizing the field. Gov Inf Q 29(3):373–382. https://doi.org/10.1016/j.giq.2011.11.005

Tavares AF, Martins J, Lameiras M (2020) Electronic participation in a comparative perspective: institutional determinants of performance. In: Rodríguez Bolívar MP, Cortés Cediel ME (Eds) Digital government and achieving E-Public participation: emerging research and opportunities, IGI Global, pp 87–123

Trischler J, Westman Trischler J (2022) Design for experience – a public service design approach in the age of digitalization. Public Manag Rev 24(8):1251–1270. https://doi.org/10.1080/14719037.2021.1899272

United Nations (2014) United Nations E-Government Survey 2014: E-Government for the future we want. United Nations Department of Economic and Social Affairs.

United Nations (2022) E-Government survey 2022: the future of digital government. United Nations Department of Economic and Social Affairs. https://desapublications.un.org/sites/default/files/publications/2022-09/Web%20version%20E-Government%202022.pdfu

van Aeken K (2017) Digital democracy in Belgium and the Netherlands: a socio-legal analysis of technologies, embedding and expectations of two fourth wave innovations. In: Prins C, Cuijpers C, Lindseth PL, Rosina M (eds) Digital democracy in a globalized world. Edward Elgar, pp 274–300

Vargo SL, Lusch RF (2004) Evolving to a new dominant logic for marketing. J Mark 68(1):1–17. https://doi.org/10.1509/jmkg.68.1.1.24036

Vertovec S (2007) Super-diversity and its implications. Ethn Racial Stud 30(6):1024–1054. https://doi.org/10.1080/01419870701599465

von der Leyen U (2019, July 16) A union that strives for more. My agenda for Europe. Political guidelines for the next European Commission 2019–2024. https://asvis.it/public/asvis2/files/Pubblicazioni/DichiarazioniVonDerLeyenSDGs.pdf

Wirtz BW, Daiser P, Binkowska B (2018) E-participation: a strategic framework. Int J Public Adm 41(1):1–12. https://doi.org/10.1080/01900692.2016.1242620

Wukich C (2021) Government social media engagement strategies and public roles. Public Perform Manag Rev 44(1):187–215. https://doi.org/10.1080/15309576.2020.1851266

Zarei F, Nik-Bakht M (2021) Citizen engagement body of knowledge – A fuzzy decision maker for index-term selection in built environment projects. Cities 112:103137. https://doi.org/10.1016/j.cities.2021.103137

**Open Access** This chapter is licensed under the terms of the Creative Commons Attribution 4.0 International License (http://creativecommons.org/licenses/by/4.0/), which permits use, sharing, adaptation, distribution and reproduction in any medium or format, as long as you give appropriate credit to the original author(s) and the source, provide a link to the Creative Commons license and indicate if changes were made.

The images or other third party material in this chapter are included in the chapter's Creative Commons license, unless indicated otherwise in a credit line to the material. If material is not included in the chapter's Creative Commons license and your intended use is not permitted by statutory regulation or exceeds the permitted use, you will need to obtain permission directly from the copyright holder.

# Chapter 4
# The Theoretical Background of Design Thinking for Public Sector Innovation

**Abstract** This chapter delves into the theoretical foundations of Design Thinking (DT) for public sector innovation, highlighting its capacity to impact organisational culture, strategic innovation, and operational processes. Emphasising a user-centric approach, the chapter explores how DT principles like abductive reasoning, prototyping, and co-design can transform public services by aligning them more closely with user needs and expectations.

**Keywords** Design thinking · Public sector innovation · User-centric design · Experimentation · Design-driven innovation

DT is a consolidated approach to innovation, recognised for being able to exert a multi-layered impact on organisational processes and operations (Elsbach and Stigliani 2018). At an organisational level, DT can influence both the individual mindset and the organisational culture, fostering a fertile environment conducive to innovation. At a strategic level, it is well recognised for its role in supporting the identification of new possibilities and pathways for innovation, aiding organisations in exploring novel areas (Brown 2008; Liedtka and Ogilvie 2011; Martin 2009). At the operational level, DT contributes to reshaping how goods and services are developed, produced, and delivered, focusing on user-centric approaches (Luca and Ulyannikova 2020). The value of DT extends to supporting organisations in engaging users in a more effective way while understanding how to leverage on their feedback and ideas across the innovation process for creating more effective and relevant solutions (Beckman and Barry 2007; Liedtka and Ogilvie 2011; Liedtka 2015; Elsbach and Stigliani 2018). In this book the DT literature is analysed to outline principles and practices that are pertinent to e-participation. This exploration aims to bridge the gap between theoretical DT concepts and their practical application in the realm of digital civic engagement, underscoring how DT can be strategically leveraged to enrich and evolve the scientific discourse on e-participation as well as its operationalisation.

© The Author(s) 2025
I. Mariani et al., *Design Thinking as a Strategic Approach to E-Participation*,
PoliMI SpringerBriefs, https://doi.org/10.1007/978-3-031-72160-1_4

## 4.1 Design Thinking Principles

Several scholars have recognised a few differentiating principles (summarised in Table 4.1) that set DT apart from other traditional approaches to innovation. A core principle is abductive reasoning (Martin 2009), which is identified as the main reasoning pattern used to approach problems, distinguishing DT from more traditional deductive and inductive logics. Abductive reasoning involves creating new hypotheses directly related to the problem, being deeply aware of the context in which the problem is situated, thereby challenging established paradigms through 'what-if' scenarios and heuristic techniques (Dorst 2011). Another defining characteristic of DT is its human-centric nature (Brown 2009; Holloway 2009), which places a strong emphasis on understanding human behaviour and needs, not only as a starting point but as a continuous focus throughout the innovation process. This approach is closely tied with the "framing and reframing" method on which DT largely relies for offering novel perspectives from which an issue can be approached and addressed (Dorst 2011; Drews 2009). Integral to this is the co-design. By actively engaging users in the innovation process, DT ensures their insights and experiences directly shape the development and outcomes of a project (Trischler et al. 2019; Deserti et al. 2020; Evans and Terrey 2016).

Further, the principle of prototyping and practical experimentation is also key, forming the bedrock of the learning and innovation process typical of DT (Dorst and Cross 2001, 2001). In particular, the relevance of early and rapid prototyping should be emphasised allowing for swift exploration and refinement of ideas (Bogers and Horst 2014, 2014; Campo Castillo and Rizzo 2020; Dorst and Cross 2001; Rhinow et al. 2012). Early and rapid prototyping serve as catalysts for running multiple cycles of development and testing with end-users and other stakeholders. DT encourages that such experimentation occurs in real contexts, where prototypes are used by end-users to assess their features against expectations and contexts of use (Evans and Terrey 2016; Trischler et al. 2019). Through the active engagement of end-users, DT ensures that in the development of solutions there is continuous adaptation and improvement aimed at better meeting user needs and expectations. The iterative and non-linear nature of DT is another foundational principle (Rizzo et al. 2018), strictly bound to development and testing for early and continuous assessment, ensuring solutions remain consistently relevant and responsive to real-world challenges and requirements effectively. Together with prototyping and practical experimentation, this principle fosters an evidence-based approach to problems and innovation. This approach underscores the importance of engaging in hands-on activities and real-world testing as a way to gain knowledge across iterative cycles (Dorst and Cross 2001). This concept is linked to the last principle, experiential learning, where learning-by-doing and learning-through-making are preferred methods for problem exploration and initiating the innovation process (Deutschmann and Botts 2015; Kolb 1984a, 1984b). This hands-on approach not only deepens understanding but also promotes creativity and innovation through direct experimentation and engagement within the problem context.

## 4.1 Design Thinking Principles

**Table 4.1** The main DT principles and their references to literature as summarised by Mortati Mariani and Rizzo (2023)

| Principle | Description | Reference |
|---|---|---|
| Abductive reasoning | Adoption of abductive reasoning as the main thought process to tackle challenges. This is distinguished from deductive and inductive logics, and is further explained through the notions of "framing and reframing", emphasising the identification of novel perspectives to tackle issues | (Dorst 2011; Drews 2009) |
| Human centricity and co-design | Innovation develops through an in-depth understanding of the needs of service users and their direct involvement as experts in the innovation process | (Brown 2009; Holloway 2009) |
| Centrality of prototyping | Experimentation is pivotal to learn-by-doing in iterative cycles. In DT, solutions are tested through "quick and dirty" prototyping, facilitating early assessment | (Dorst and Cross, 2001) |
| Experimentation in real contexts | Prototypes are used and assessed by end-users in real contexts to assess their features against expectations and contexts of use | (Evans and Terrey 2016; Trischler et al. 2019) |
| Iterative and non-linear process | Early and fast prototyping through iterative development and testing cycles with end-users and other actors are fundamental for fast learning and consequent improvement of solutions | (Rizzo et al. 2018) |
| Experiential learning | Learning-by-doing and learning-through-making are the preferred ways to explore problems and kick-start the innovation process | (Deutschmann and Botts 2015; Kolb 1984b, 1984a) |

Initially emerging in the USA as a method to better align business objectives with customer desires (Brown 2009), DT is currently increasingly valued as an approach to public sector innovation. As early as 2013, the expert group on public sector innovation of the European Commission argued for the urgent need to reinforce innovation within the public sector (2013). This call to action was not just about unlocking productivity and efficiency but also about discovering alternative ways to respond to societal challenges through the innovation of processes (with an internal focus) and services (with an external focus). Since then, the development of citizen-centred services, including through digital platforms, and the fostering of effective citizen engagement have become central to public sector innovation (Organisation for Economic Co-operation and Development 2001; Khan and Krishnan 2021; OECD 2009). This evolution is meant to culminate in a new entrepreneurial culture for public managers, a change in mindset, and a more personalised response to public issues. This trajectory has been recently consolidated by the principles set forth in the

2017 Tallinn Declaration[1] (2017), which pointed out the need of user-centricity in designing better public services and rethinking existing procedures and operational workflows.

In practical terms, the drive to modernise government processes through DT is witnessed by the proliferation of Public Sector Innovation (PSI) labs. With more than 60 labs spread across the EU member states (Fuller and Lochard 2016; Puttick 2014, pp. 6–7), these 'islands of experimentation' (Tõnurist et al. 2017, p. 8) have been pioneering new methods to revolutionise public participation and the design and delivery of public services (Craft and Howlett 2013). A study of 20 PSI labs conducted by McGann and colleagues (2018) highlighted that around half of these labs declared to be design-led, with DT being predominantly adopted in labs within public administrations and in those funded by governments. In such contexts, co-design is adopted as an approach to involve users in governmental processes. Additional knowledge comes from Kimbell's (Kimbell 2015) examination of Policy Lab UK, which highlighted the impact of applying DT in the public sector, noting (i) a shift in focus towards people and their experiences, fostering new approaches and reorienting public services and policy development based on real-life impacts; (ii) the temporary flattening of hierarchies through co-design, fostering spaces for collective exploration and ideation; and (iii) the enabling of people from inside and outside the government to collaborate on public issues, by establishing a shared language, equal participation, and constructive acknowledgment of differences. Studies on PSI labs have demonstrated that their status of experimental environments successfully fostered the development of new capabilities for subsequent integration into routine operations, thereby enhancing organisational learning (Kimbell 2015; Bailey and Lloyd 2016).

Against this backdrop, DT garnered increasing recognition and value among public organisations, who are actively integrating its core principles into their processes (Brown and Wyatt 2010; Liedtka 2015; Deserti and Rizzo 2014; Rizzo and Deserti 2018).

## 4.2 Design Thinking Practices

The principles of DT can be closely associated with relevant practices in the field. This association is rooted in the foundational elements of DT. For instance, the principle of human centricity is fundamental in practices like co-production, where understanding user needs is crucial. Similarly, the iterative and non-linear nature of DT is mirrored in the continuous cycles of experimentation and prototyping, fostering a culture of adaptation and learning. This symbiotic relationship between

---

[1] The main principles for the successful implementation of digital public services are listed as: digital by default, citizen-centricity, inclusiveness, trustworthiness, accessibility, openness, transparency and interoperability.

## 4.2 Design Thinking Practices

DT principles and practices underscores its effectiveness in addressing complex problems through innovative solutions.

Figure 4.1 connects DT principles with DT practices. Table 4.2 highlights how each principle underpins DT practices, establishing a logical framework for understanding their relationship. In the remainder of this paragraph, each practice is described.

**Meaning creation and sense-making.** In the innovation management literature, meaning creation and sense-making are processes integral to generating value, particularly by leveraging intangible benefits like symbolic and emotional relationships with products and services (Dell'Era and Verganti 2007). This involves designers focusing on redefining innovation problems through direct user research, where qualitative data is extracted from observations of daily behaviours. These observations are transformed into insights that delve into the deeper motivations behind people's actions (Dong and MacDonald 2017; Grönroos and Voima 2013). These practices, informed by an understanding of the hidden dynamics of socio-cultural models, are instrumental in guiding the development of new products and services, aligning them

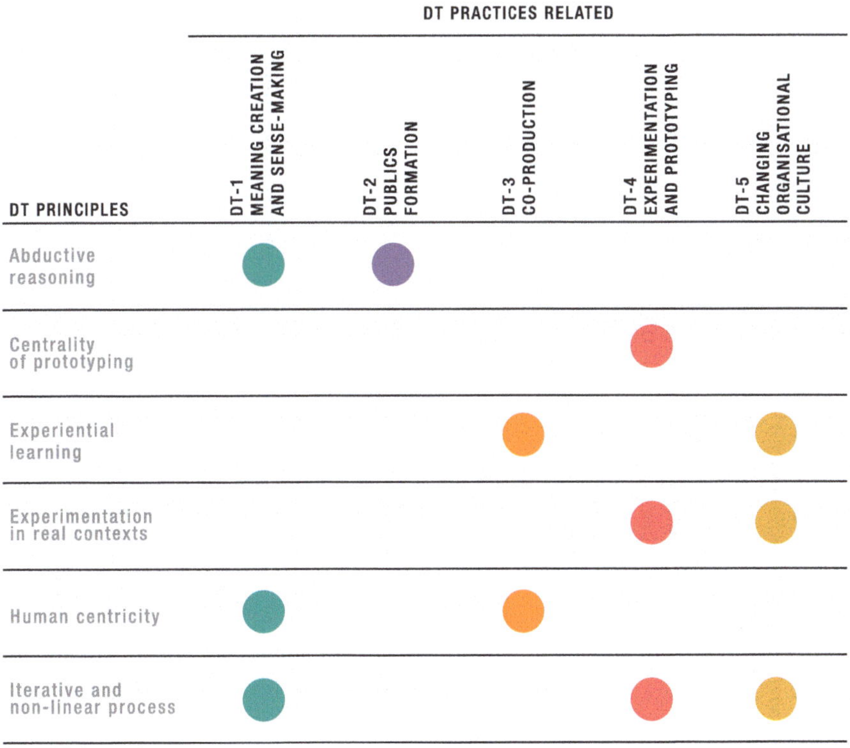

**Fig. 4.1** Mapping DT principles against DT practices

**Table 4.2** DT principles feeding DT practices and relevant references

| DT practices | References | DT principles | Description |
|---|---|---|---|
| DT-1: Meaning creation and sense-making | (Al-Kodmany 2001; Alshuwaikhat and Nkwenti 2002; Bogers et al. 2010; Dong and MacDonald 2017; Dorst 2011; Drews 2009; Grönroos and Voima 2013; Junginger 2014; Kimbell 2015; Lewis et al. 2020; Liedtka 2015; Mazé 2014; Venturini et al. 2015) | Abductive reasoning | Abductive reasoning refers to a designerly way of interpreting and making sense of diverse perspectives and information that can be multilayered, ambiguous or tangled. This approach facilitates the creation of meaningful solutions by deeply understanding and interpreting various perspectives and information. It regards how to approach complex problems to unravel and turn them into meaningful insights, laying the groundwork for creating solutions that are deeply grounded in real-world context.. This principle is key in the process of building meanings and developing insightful hypotheses on which to build the development of meaningful and desirable solutions |
| | | Human centricity | This principle refers to the need to put real human experiences and needs at the centre. It brings a human-focused lens to the sense-making process, ensuring solutions are empathetically aligned with user requirements. Human centricity ensures that the sense-making activity is always rooted in real issues, experiences, and needs. It sets the ground of a design that is directly informed by user insights, making the design process more relevant and impactful |
| | | Iterative and non-linear process | This principle supports the idea that understanding and sense-making are not a straight path but a dynamic and adaptive one, where ideas and solutions can be refined in response to new insights, perspectives, and feedback. This principle highlights the fluid nature of knowledge development, allowing for the inclusion of emerging viewpoints, shifts in understanding, and changes in context. By embracing this iterative approach, it ensures that meaning creation and sense-making processes are continuously aligned with and responsive to evolving user needs and environmental factors, fostering solutions that are consistently relevant, effective, and resonant with the intended audience |

(continued)

## 4.2 Design Thinking Practices

Table 4.2 (continued)

| DT practices | References | DT principles | Description |
|---|---|---|---|
| DT-2: Publics formation | (Al-Kodmany 2001; Alshuwaikhat and Nkwenti 2002; Björgvinsson et al. 2012; Chuan et al. 2021; Dantec and DiSalvo 2013; Deserti et al. 2020; DiSalvo 2012, 2010; Egenhoefer 2017; A. Escobar 2018; European Commission et al. 2019; Kimbell 2015; Kimbell et al. 2022; Kuijer 2014; Le Dantec 2016; Sangiorgi and Prendiville 2017; Saward 2021; Venturini et al. 2015; Vink et al. 2021) | Abductive reasoning | Abductive reasoning facilitates the formation of insightful hypotheses about the needs and expectations of diverse public groups. This principle is instrumental in exploring the complexities of multiple stakeholders with multilayered dynamics. It supports the identification of plausible assumptions from available data as a first step for then identifying and effectively engaging with different publics. It enables a deeper understanding of varied groups, laying the groundwork for meaningful engagement and for informing the design of tailored and more desirable solutions. This approach ensures that the formation of publics is grounded in an in-depth comprehension of the varied perspectives and needs which are present in the society, thus leading to more targeted and impactful public engagement strategies |
| DT-3: Co-production | (Bekkers et al. 2013; Bentzen et al. 2020; Blomkamp 2018; Deserti et al. 2020; Durose and Richardson 2015; Jukić et al. 2019; Kaletka et al. 2018; Khan and Krishnan 2021; Linders 2012; Liu 2021; Osborne et al. 2016; Seravalli et al. 2017; Strokosch and Osborne 2020) | Human centricity | Human centricity is at the heart of co-production, recognising the relevance of aligning with users' and stakeholders' perspectives to develop truly effective and desirable solutions. This principle underscores the importance of deeply engaging with users throughout the design process, ensuring their needs and expectations are at the forefront across the different stages. By adopting a human-centred approach, co-production activities become more than just collaborative efforts; they transform into fertile settings where users' insights are intertwined into the fabric of the solution. This alignment guarantees that the outcomes are not only relevant but also resonate strongly with the users, leading to solutions that effectively address challenges |

(continued)

Table 4.2 (continued)

| DT practices | References | DT principles | Description |
|---|---|---|---|
| | | Experiential learning | Experiential learning is a central principle to co-production since it champions active, hands-on participation in the design process. This principle enriches co-production by fostering a learning environment where users are directly engaged in the design process, in a setting that is open to interaction and to receive feedback. In co-production, experiential learning goes beyond mere participation; it encourages a shared learning experience, where insights, skills, and expertise are collectively built and exchanged. This leads to solutions that are not only innovative but also deeply rooted in the practical knowledge and experiences of those involved, making them more relevant, effective, and embraced by the community |
| DT-4: Experimentation and prototyping | Coughlan et al., 2007; McGann et al., 2018; Rhinow et al., 2012; Sanders & Stappers, 2014; Schmittinger et al., 2020; Tõnurist et al., 2017; Villa Alvarez et al., 2020; Zimmerman et al., 2007) | Centrality of prototyping | Prototyping is a core element of co-production, enabling the physical exploration of tangible, interactive models of ideas and concepts, allowing for their physical exploration and refinement. Prototyping serves as a bridge between theoretical concepts and practical applications, enabling the direct testing and validation of design ideas in real-world context. It allows users and designers to interact with prototypes, gaining insights and feedback that inform further development. This hands-on approach not only deepens the understanding of the potential solutions and their respective challenges but also leverages the diverse skills and experiences of all participants involved. By emphasising the centrality of prototyping, this principle ensures that the experimentation process is dynamic, collaborative, and geared towards innovation. It enables the iterative evolution of ideas, transforming abstract concepts into practical, testable, and ultimately more effective solutions |

(continued)

## 4.2 Design Thinking Practices

**Table 4.2** (continued)

| DT practices | References | DT principles | Description |
|---|---|---|---|
| | | Experimentation in real contexts | Experimentation in real contexts builds upon the necessity of testing and validating prototypes and design solutions in actual, real-world environments. It ensures that the ideas developed are not only theoretically sound but also practically feasible and effective when implemented in real-life scenarios. As such, it provides a crucial testing ground, where the practical implications, usability, and results of the solution designed can be observed and evaluated. This approach allows for an evidence-based understanding of how solutions perform in real settings, leading to more informed and effective designs. By grounding the experimentation process in real-world contexts, this principle ensures that the outcomes of the design process are not only innovative but also practically viable, relevant, and responsive to the actual needs and conditions of the intended users |
| | | Iterative and non-linear process | Iteration is key in prototyping; as feedback is gathered, the process cycles back to refinement and further experimentation. This principle underlines the importance of a flexible and adaptive approach to design, where feedback plays a critical role in informing and refining prototypes. In this iterative process, prototypes are not static; they evolve continuously based on real-world feedback and insights gained from each cycle of testing and experimentation. This approach allows for a dynamic development process that is adaptable to changing needs and contexts. By embracing this iterative and non-linear approach, experimentation and prototyping shape as continual learning and adaptation, ensuring that the final solutions are not only innovative but also highly tuned to the specific requirements and feedback of users |

(continued)

Table 4.2 (continued)

| DT practices | References | DT principles | Description |
|---|---|---|---|
| DT-5: Changing organisational culture | (Beckman and Barry 2007; Deserti and Rizzo 2014; Rizzo et al. 2017; Elsbach and Stigliani 2018; Geraldi and Söderlund 2016; Kimbell 2015; Payne, Storbacka, and Frow 2008; Coughlan, Suri, and Canales 2007) | Experimentation in real contexts | Experimentation in real contexts is strictly related with the transformative impact of real-world experimentation on organisational norms and cultures. By engaging in experimentation within actual contexts, organisations are compelled to confront and challenge their established norms and practices. This process not only tests the viability of new ideas and approaches but also fosters a culture of adaptability and innovation: they are encouraged to step out of their traditional boundaries and comfort zones, exploring and embracing new ways of thinking and working. Such real-context experimentation acts as a catalyst for cultural change, pushing organisations to evolve and adapt in response to the dynamics of the context |
| | | Iterative and non-linear process | Iterative and non-linear process underlines the importance of adopting a flexible, adaptive approach, which is pivotal for fostering a culture of continuous improvement. By facilitating a continuous evolution of ideas and strategies, with regular incorporation of feedback, learning, and refinement, it encourages a shift from rigid, linear processes towards embracing a more dynamic way of working. As such, this principle relates to a culture that values learning from both failures and successes, recognising adaptability as essential in addressing complexities and changing circumstances. It cultivates an innovative mindset within the organisation, where experimentation and continual learning are integral components |
| | | Experiential learning | Experiential learning plays a crucial role in driving cultural change by highlighting the importance of learning from direct experiences and interactions. It is instrumental in transforming organisational culture, fostering a mindset that values continual learning, experimentation, and innovation. It encourages to embrace and prioritise hands-on experiences as a fundamental way of understanding and implementing change |

more closely with the user's values and needs (Bogers et al. 2010; Dorst 2011; Drews 2009; Junginger 2014; Kimbell 2015; Lewis et al. 2020). Qualitatively studying and interpreting people's needs is critical for design thinkers, providing input and experiences that shape the direction of innovative solutions bearing value for the context in which they are enacted (Bogers et al. 2010). This process also encourages the reduction of individual cognitive biases through rigorous, user-focused research (Liedtka 2015). In this context, data visualisation supports decision-making by analysing and visualising complex information (Al-Kodmany 2001; Alshuwaikhat and Nkwenti 2002; Venturini et al. 2015). Thus, in DT, the process of meaning creation and sense-making extends from observing and empathising with users to creating meaningful, value-driven innovations, and it is marked by a deep engagement with the qualitative aspects of user experience, and framing and reframing of challenges.

**Publics formation supporting awareness and plurality.** The concept of public formation is relevant for its generative role in the creation of publics (Le Dantec 2016). Rooted in the idea of infrastructuring, public formation in DT involves identifying and shaping social and material interdependencies among community members, thereby forming a cohesive public (Björgvinsson et al. 2012; Dantec and DiSalvo 2013). This process facilitates the identification of needs and framing of problems, supports the definition of potential future consequences, and encourages the negotiation of multiple perspectives. Data visualisation methods play a supportive role in this process (Al-Kodmany 2001; Alshuwaikhat and Nkwenti 2002), facilitating clarification and sometimes provoking controversies to stimulate generative discussions (DiSalvo 2010, 2012; Venturini et al. 2015). The rich literature in design discusses the social and political implications of designing, while taking into account its uneven and unequal effects. Examples of these reflections span across areas like democratic design (Saward 2021), urban innovation and city planning (Chuan et al. 2021), policy-making (European Commission et al. 2019), and science, technology, and innovation policy-making (Deserti et al. 2020). In these fields, DT is acknowledged for providing agency to those affected by incorporating diverse perspectives and stimulating reflection in the public discourse (Escobar 2018). Practices like design for sustainability are centred on engaging publics in generating and assessing new designs that promote ecological sustainability (Egenhoefer 2017), integrating insights from social and behavioural sciences (Kuijer 2014). In this context, designers act as cultural mediators, with DT playing a pivotal role in influencing public discourse (Kimbell 2015; Kimbell et al. 2022), through the creation of environments, experiences, artefacts, and communication systems. Service and systems design also focus on public formation by engaging stakeholder ecosystems for systemic change (Sangiorgi and Prendiville 2017). These research areas acknowledge that multi-actor service systems are influenced by institutional frameworks and other interdependencies, thus requiring attention on these aspects for lasting change in practice (Vink et al. 2021).

**Co-production with citizens.** Co-production with citizens describes a transformative process where inputs from individuals external to an organisation are transformed into valuable goods and services (Ostrom 1996). This concept redefines the relationship between public services' provider and the beneficiary, repositioning the latter not as a passive recipient but as an active co-producer. Co-production can occur at individual, group, or collective levels, each featuring distinct characteristics and implications (Grönroos and Voima 2013). Individual co-production indicates situations in which an individual is in the meanwhile producer and beneficiary (e.g., home-schooling services); group co-production describes situations where a specific group of citizens is both producer and beneficiary (e.g., residents of a neighbourhood engaging in watch schemes); collective co-production sees a group of citizens as providers of a service (e.g., time-banking) but the beneficiaries are the wider community.

This approach has been discussed in the literature, covering various dimensions of social innovation and co-creation (Bekkers et al. 2013; Deserti et al. 2020; Jukić et al. 2019; Kaletka et al. 2018; Linders 2012; Osborne et al. 2016). Co-creation and co-production are seen as a means to encourage and foster public engagement in public service development and policy design (Blomkamp 2018; Durose and Richardson 2015; Seravalli et al. 2017), and is recognised as integral to processes encouraging collective participation (Craft and Howlett 2013; Krogh et al. 2015; McGann et al. 2018; Rhinow et al. 2012; Sanders and Stappers 2014; Schmittinger et al. 2020; Strokosch and Osborne 2020; Tõnurist et al. 2017). Co-production in DT is thus recognised as a strategy for enhancing public engagement and fostering innovative solutions in public sector policy-making, service design, and delivery.

**Experimenting and prototyping.** Experimentation and prototyping are increasingly being adopted by governments as DT methods also to test new methods to more actively engage citizens in public services delivery. Among these approaches, prototyping has been gaining significant attention as a means for encouraging public participation in service development and policy-making (Kimbell and Bailey 2017; McGann et al. 2018; Villa Alvarez et al. 2020). Described as an iterative process of development and testing, it regards the creation of tangible representations (prototypes) that serve as tools for learning, refining ideas, and facilitating communication within teams and with external stakeholders (Blomkvist 2014; Floyd 1984; Gero 1990). As such, prototypes often function as 'boundary objects' (Rhinow et al. 2012) that can facilitate dialogue across domains of expertise and practice, thus helping to overcome implementation barriers. The use of prototypes in experimental settings can help to mitigate fear of failure, and allow for the validation of hypotheses before extensive deployment (Sanders and Stappers 2014; Schmittinger et al. 2020; Villa Alvarez et al. 2020). As concretisations of an envisioned future, prototypes can bridge the realm of possibilities with actionable directions for experimentation (Zimmerman et al. 2007). This approach to prototyping supports collaborative problem-solving, blending knowledge from different fields and promoting organisational change towards innovative solutions (Bogers and Horst 2014; Coughlan et al. 2007; Sanders and Stappers 2014; Schmittinger et al. 2020). Moreover, the rise of public sector innovation labs exemplifies the application of these prototyping techniques in real-world policy contexts, offering a fertile ground for experimenting with design thinking in policy-making (McGann et al. 2018; Tõnurist et al. 2017).

**Changing organisational culture.** Public organisations are increasingly integrating DT and co-creation methodologies to spur innovation and facilitate transformative change. DT, in particular, is being recognised for its capacity to foster socio-cultural and political transformations, enabling deeper citizen engagement within the practices of public institutions (Kimbell 2015). However, integrating DT into public sector operations requires significant shifts in organisational culture and mindset. This change extends beyond top-down leadership, demanding active participation and contribution from all organisational levels (Deserti and Rizzo 2014; Elsbach and Stigliani 2018). Such transformations represent a necessary step for embedding innovative and participatory approaches within public organisations and their processes, aligning them with contemporary demands for collaborative and user-centred governance. Literature has highlighted the learning processes inherent in innovation, stressing the role of DT in embedding new ways of thinking and working (Beckman and Barry 2007; Payne et al. 2008). Prototypes can serve as triggers for supporting this learning while triggering behavioural and organisational change, demonstrating the practical implications of adopting DT approaches (Coughlan et al. 2007). These studies collectively underscore the pivotal role of DT in driving and sustaining organisational change, reshaping traditional public sector practices into more dynamic, inclusive, and innovative operations.

Building on this, the possibility to complement and enhance e-participation through DT (Junginger 2013) is an opportunity to extend beyond tech-driven or market-inspired innovation in the public sector. For instance, it can contribute to mitigating the gap between policies and how they are experienced by citizens as they interact with public services (Mintrom and Thomas 2018), offering a different way to make policy tangible (Bason 2014). Nevertheless, public innovation that adopts a citizen-centred and value-focused model represents a profound shift from traditional public governance structures. This shift demands substantial transformation, posing a challenge to the prevailing command-and-control dynamics characteristic of current hierarchical public institutions.

**Funding** Some of the reasoning presented in this work derive from knowledge and insights from the project "AI4GOV, Artificial Intelligence for Public Services", Action No. 2020-EU-IA-0064, co-financed by the EU CEF Telecom (No. INEA/CEF/ICT/A2020/2265375) [ai4gov-hub.eu; ai4gov-master.eu]. The opinions expressed herewith are solely of the authors and do not necessarily reflect the point of view of any EU institution.

# References

Al-Kodmany K (2001) Visualization tools and methods for participatory planning and design. J Urban Technol 8(2):1–37. https://doi.org/10.1080/106307301316904772

Alshuwaikhat HM, Nkwenti DI (2002) Visualizing decisionmaking: perspectives on collaborative and participative approach to sustainable urban planning and management. Environ Plann B Plann Des 29(4):513–531. https://doi.org/10.1068/b12818

Bailey J, Lloyd P (2016) The introduction of design to policymaking: policy lab and the UK government. In: Proceedings of DRS 2016, design research society 50th anniversary conference. Design research society, vol. 1, pp 3619–3635. https://doi.org/10.21606/drs.2016.314

Bason C (2014) Design attitude as an innovation catalyst. In: Ansell C, Torfing J (eds) Public innovation through collaboration and design. Routledge, pp 227–246

Beckman SL, Barry M (2007) Innovation as a learning process: embedding design thinking. Calif Manage Rev 50(1):25–56. https://doi.org/10.2307/41166415

Bekkers V, Tummers LG, Voorberg WH (2013) From public innovation to social innovation in the public sector: A literature review of relevant drivers and barriers. Erasmus University Rotterdam, Rotterdam

Bentzen TØ, Sørensen E, Torfing J (2020) Strengthening public service production, administrative problem solving, and political leadership through co-creation of innovative public value outcomes. The Innovation Journal: The Public Sector Innovation Journal, 25(1):1–28.

Björgvinsson E, Ehn P, Hillgren P-A (2012) Agonistic participatory design: working with marginalised social movements. CoDesign 8(2–3):127–144. https://doi.org/10.1080/15710882.2012.672577

Blomkamp E (2018) The promise of co-design for public policy. Aust J Public Adm 77(4):729–743. https://doi.org/10.1111/1467-8500.12310

Blomkvist J (2014) Representing future situations of service: prototyping in service design. Doctoral thesis, comprehensive summary. Linköping Studies in Arts and Sciences. Linköping University Electronic Press, Linköping. Retrieved from DiVA

Bogers M, Afuah A, Bastian B (2010) Users as innovators: a review, critique, and future research directions. J Manag 36(4):857–875. https://doi.org/10.1177/0149206309353944

Bogers M, Horst W (2014) Collaborative prototyping: cross-fertilization of knowledge in prototype-driven problem solving. J Prod Innov Manag 31(4):744–764. https://doi.org/10.1111/jpim.12121

Brown T (2008) Design thinking. Harv Bus Rev 86(6):84–92

Brown T (2009) Change by design. HarperCollins, New York

Brown T, Wyatt J (2010) Design thinking for social innovation. Dev Outreach 12(1):29–43. https://doi.org/10.1596/1020-797X_12_1_29

Campo Castillo A, Rizzo F (2020) Prototyping in design for policy: uncertainty and policymakers' engagement. In: ICERI2020 Proceedings. IATED, pp 4512–4522. https://doi.org/10.21125/iceri.2020.0993

Chuan L, Rausell-Köster P, Morelli N, Simeone L, Azohar H, Concilio G, et al. (2021) Designscapes: white paper on design enabled innovation in Europe. Anci Toscana Associazione, Florence. https://doi.org/10.13140/RG.2.2.17559.09127

Coughlan P, Suri JF, Canales K (2007) Prototypes as (design) tools for behavioral and organizational change: a design-based approach to help organizations change work behaviors. J Appl Behav Sci 43(1):122–134. https://doi.org/10.1177/0021886306297722

Craft J, Howlett M (2013) The dual dynamics of policy advisory systems: the impact of externalization and politicization on policy advice. Policy Soc 32(3):187–197. https://doi.org/10.1016/j.polsoc.2013.07.001

Dantec CAL, DiSalvo C (2013) Infrastructuring and the formation of publics in participatory design. Soc Stud Sci 43(2):241–264. https://doi.org/10.1177/0306312712471581

Dell'Era C, Verganti R (2007) Strategies of innovation and imitation of product languages*. J Prod Innov Manag 24(6):580–599. https://doi.org/10.1111/j.1540-5885.2007.00273.x

Deserti A, Rizzo F (2014) Design and organizational change in the public sector. Des Manag J 9(1):85–97. https://doi.org/10.1111/dmj.12013

Deserti A, Rizzo F, Smallman M (2020) Experimenting with co-design in STI policy making. Policy Des Pract 3(2):135–149. https://doi.org/10.1080/25741292.2020.1764692

Deutschmann M, Botts M (2015) Experiential learning through the design thinking technique. In: Taras V, Gonzalez-Perez MA (eds), The Palgrave handbook of experiential learning in international business. Palgrave Macmillan London, UK, pp 449–463. https://doi.org/10.1057/9781137467720_26

# References

DiSalvo C (2010) Design, democracy and agonistic pluralism. In: DRS2010 RESEARCH PAPERS. Presented at the DRS2010: design and complexity, Montreal, Canada. https://dl.designresearchsociety.org/drs-conference-papers/drs2010/researchpapers/31

DiSalvo C (2012) Adversarial design. MIT Press. https://doi.org/10.7551/mitpress/8732.001.0001

Dong A, MacDonald E (2017) From observations to insights: the hilly road to value creation. Analysing design thinking: studies of cross-cultural co-creation. CRC Press, London, UK, pp 465–482

Dorst K (2011) The core of 'design thinking' and its application. Interpret Des Think 32(6):521–532. https://doi.org/10.1016/j.destud.2011.07.006

Dorst K, Cross N (2001) Creativity in the design process: co-evolution of problem–solution. Des Stud 22(5):425–437. https://doi.org/10.1016/S0142-694X(01)00009-6

Drews C (2009) Unleashing the full potential of design thinking as a business method. Des Manag Rev 20(3):38–44. https://doi.org/10.1111/j.1948-7169.2009.00020.x

Durose C, Richardson L (2015) Designing public policy for co-production: Theory, practice and change. Policy Press, Bristol, UK. https://doi.org/10.2307/j.ctt1t896qg

Egenhoefer RB (2017) Routledge handbook of sustainable design. Routledge, London, UK

Elsbach KD, Stigliani I (2018) Design thinking and organizational culture: a review and framework for future research. J Manag 44(6):2274–2306. https://doi.org/10.1177/0149206317744252

Escobar, A. (2018). Designs for the pluriverse: radical interdependence, autonomy, and the making of worlds. Duke University Press.

European Commission—Directorate-General for Research and Innovation (2013) Powering European Public Sector Innovation: towards a New Architecture. Report of the Expert Group on Public Sector Innovation. European Commission—Directorate-General for Research and Innovation. https://doi.org/10.2777/51054

European Commission, Directorate-General for Research and Innovation, & Merkel W (2019) Past, present and future of democracy—policy review. Publications Office of the European Union, Luxembourg. https://doi.org/10.2777/281418

Evans M, Terrey N (2016) Co-design with citizens and stakeholders. Evidence-Based Policy Making in the Social Sciences: Methods That Matter, 243.

Floyd C (1984) A systematic look at prototyping. In: Budde R, Kuhlenkamp K, Mathiassen L, Züllighoven H (eds) Approaches to prototyping, Springer Berlin Heidelberg, Berlin, Heidelberg. pp 1–18

Fuller M, Lochard A (2016) Public policy labs in European Union members states (Other No. LB-NA-28044-EN-N). Publications Office of the European Union, Luxembourg (Luxembourg). https://doi.org/10.2788/799175

Geraldi J, Söderlund J (2016) Project studies and engaged scholarship: Directions towards contextualized and reflexive research on projects. Int J Managing Proj Bus 9(4):767–797. https://doi.org/10.1108/IJMPB-02-2016-0016

Gero JS (1990) Design prototypes: a knowledge representation schema for design. AI Mag 11(4):26. https://doi.org/10.1609/aimag.v11i4.854

Grönroos C, Voima P (2013) Critical service logic: making sense of value creation and co-creation. J Acad Mark Sci 41(2):133–150. https://doi.org/10.1007/s11747-012-0308-3

Holloway M (2009) How tangible is your strategy? How design thinking can turn your strategy into reality. J Bus Strateg 30(2/3):50–56. https://doi.org/10.1108/02756660910942463

Jukić T, Pevcin P, Benčina J, Dečman M, Vrbek S (2019) Collaborative innovation in public administration: theoretical background and research trends of co-production and co-creation. Adm Sci 9(4). https://doi.org/10.3390/admsci9040090

Junginger S (2013) Design and innovation in the public sector: matters of design in policy-making and policy implementation. Annu Rev Policy Des 1(1):1–11

Junginger, S. (2014). Towards policy-making as designing: policy-making beyond problem-solving and decision-making. In Bason C (ed) Design for policy. Routledge, London, UK, pp 57–69. https://doi.org/10.4324/9781315576640

Kaletka C, Eckhardt J, Krüger D (2018) Theoretical framework and tools for understanding co-creation in contexts (No. D1.3). https://ec.europa.eu/research/participants/documents/downloadPublic?documentIds=080166e5bed185fb&appId=PPGMS

Khan A, Krishnan S (2021) Citizen engagement in co-creation of e-government services: a process theory view from a meta-synthesis approach. Internet Res 31(4):1318–1375. https://doi.org/10.1108/INTR-03-2020-0116

Kimbell L (2015) Applying design approaches to policy making: discovering policy lab. University of Brighton, Brighton, UK

Kimbell L, Bailey J (2017) Prototyping and the new spirit of policy-making. CoDesign 13(3):214–226. https://doi.org/10.1080/15710882.2017.1355003

Kimbell L, Richardson L, Mazé R, Durose, C (2022) Design for public policy: embracing uncertainty and hybridity in mapping future research. In: DRS2022: Bilbao vol. 25. https://doi.org/10.21606/drs.2022.303

Kolb DA (1984a). Experiential learning as the science of learning and development. Englewood Cliffs NPH

Kolb DA (1984b) Experience as the source of learning and development. Prentice Hall, Upper Sadle River

Krogh PG, Markussen T, Bang AL (2015) Ways of drifting—five methods of experimentation in research through design. In Chakrabarti A (ed) ICoRD'15—Research into design across boundaries volume 1. India, Springer India New Delhi, pp 39–50. https://doi.org/10.1007/978-81-322-2232-3_4

Kuijer L (2014) Implications of social practice theory for sustainable design. PhD Dissertation. Delft, The Netherlands, Delft University of Technology, Retrieved from https://https://doi.org/10.4233/uuid:d1662dc5-9706-4bb5-933b-75704c72ba30

Le Dantec CA (2016) Designing publics. MIT Press, Cambridge, MA

Lewis JM, McGann M, Blomkamp E (2020) When design meets power: design thinking, public sector innovation and the politics of policymaking. Policy Polit 48(1):111–130. https://doi.org/10.1332/030557319X15579230420081

Liedtka J (2015) Perspective: linking design thinking with innovation outcomes through cognitive bias reduction. J Prod Innov Manag 32(6):925–938. https://doi.org/10.1111/jpim.12163

Liedtka J, Ogilvie T (2011) Designing for growth: a design thinking tool kit for managers. Columbia University Press, New York, NY

Linders D (2012) From e-government to we-government: DEFINING a typology for citizen coproduction in the age of social media. Social Media in Government—Selections from the 12th Annual International Conference on Digital Government Research (dg.o2011) 29(4):446–454. https://doi.org/10.1016/j.giq.2012.06.003

Luca EJ, Ulyannikova Y (2020) Towards a user-centred systematic review service: the transformative power of service design thinking. J Aust Libr Inf Assoc 69(3):357–374. https://doi.org/10.1080/24750158.2020.1760506

Martin RL (2009) The design of business: why design thinking is the next competitive advantage. Harvard Business Press, Cambridge, MA

Mazé R (2014) Our Common Future? Political questions for designing social innovation. In: Lim Y, Niedderer K, Redström J, Stolterman E, & Valtonen A (Eds), Proceedings of DRS2014 International Conference: Design's Big Debates. Design Research Society. https://dl.designresearchsociety.org/drs-conferencepapers/drs2014/researchpapers/41/

McGann M, Blomkamp E, Lewis JM (2018) The rise of public sector innovation labs: experiments in design thinking for policy. Policy Sci 51(3):249–267. https://doi.org/10.1007/s11077-018-9315-7

Mintrom M, Thomas M (2018) Improving commissioning through design thinking. Policy Des Pract 1(4):310–322. https://doi.org/10.1080/25741292.2018.1551756

Mortati M, Mariani I, Rizzo F (2023) How design thinking can support the establishment of an EU GovTech ecosystem. In: De Sainz Molestina D, Galluzzo L, Rizzo F, Spallazzo D (Eds)

# References

IASDR 2023: life-changing design, DRS, Milano, Italy, (pp. 1–29). Presented at the IASDR 2023: life-changing design. https://doi.org/10.21606/iasdr.2023.356

OECD (2009) Focus on citizens. https://doi.org/10.1787/9789264048874-en

Osborne SP, Radnor Z, Strokosch K (2016) Co-Production and the Co-Creation of value in public services: a suitable case for treatment? Public Manag Rev 18(5):639–653. https://doi.org/10.1080/14719037.2015.1111927

Ostrom E (1996) Crossing the great divide: coproduction, synergy, and development. World Dev 24(6):1073–1087. https://doi.org/10.1016/0305-750X(96)00023-X

Organisation for Economic Co-operation and Development (2001) Citizens as partners: information, consultation and public participation economic co-operation and development in policy-making. Organisation for Economic Co-operation and Development.

Payne AF, Storbacka K, Frow P (2008) Managing the co-creation of value. J Acad Mark Sci 36(1):83–96. https://doi.org/10.1007/s11747-007-0070-0

Puttick R (2014) Innovation Teams and Labs: a practice guide. NESTA, London, 12. http://www.nesta.org.uk/publications/innovation-teams-and-labs-practice-guide

Rhinow H, Köppen E, Meinel C (2012) Design prototypes as boundary objects in innovation processes. In: Israsena P, Tangsantikul J, Durling D (eds) Research: uncertainty contradiction value—DRS International Conference 2012, pp 1581–1590. Presented at the DRS International Conference 2012, Bangkok, Thailand, 1–4 July. https://dl.designresearchsociety.org/drs-conference-papers/drs2012/researchpapers/116

Rizzo F, Deserti A, & Cobanli O (2017) Introducing Design Thinking in Social Innovation and in Public Sector: A design-based learning framework. Eur Public Soc Innov Rev, 2(1):127–143.

Rizzo F, Deserti A (2018) The "real" vs the "ideal" process of social innovation development: a case-based analysis. In: 13th international forum on knowledge asset dynamics. Delft University of Technology, pp 693–704

Rizzo F, Deserti A, Crabu S, Smallman M, Hjort J, Hansen SJ, Menichinelli M (2018) Co-creation in RRI practices and STI policies (No. D1.2). https://ec.europa.eu/research/participants/documents/downloadPublic?documentIds=080166e5bedc3a0d&appId=PPGMS

Sanders EB-N, Stappers PJ (2014) Probes, toolkits and prototypes: three approaches to making in codesigning. CoDesign 10(1):5–14. https://doi.org/10.1080/15710882.2014.888183

Sangiorgi D, Prendiville A (2017) Designing for service: key issues and new directions. Bloomsbury Publishing, London, UK and New York, NY

Saward M (2021) Democratic design. Oxford University Press, Oxford, UK

Schmittinger F, Rizzo F, Deserti A (2020) Experimenting design thinking in RRI as a model of knowledge exchange between bottom-up initiatives and policy making. In: 15th International forum on knowledge asset Dynamics Arts for Business Institute, pp 689–704

Seravalli A, Agger Eriksen M, Hillgren P-A (2017) Co-design in co-production processes: jointly articulating and appropriating infrastructuring and commoning with civil servants. CoDesign 13(3):187–201. https://doi.org/10.1080/15710882.2017.1355004

Strokosch K, Osborne SP (2020) Co-experience, co-production and co-governance: an ecosystem approach to the analysis of value creation. Policy Polit 48(3):425–442. https://doi.org/10.1332/030557320X15857337955214

Tallinn Declaration (2017) Tallinn Declaration on eGovernment at the ministerial meeting during Estonian presidency of the council of the EU on 6 October 2017. https://ec.europa.eu/newsroom/document.cfm?doc_id=47559

Tõnurist P, Kattel R, Lember V (2017) Innovation labs in the public sector: what they are and what they do? Public Manag Rev 19(10):1455–1479. https://doi.org/10.1080/14719037.2017.1287939

Trischler J, Dietrich T, Rundle-Thiele S (2019) Co-design: from expert- to user-driven ideas in public service design. Public Manag Rev 21(11):1595–1619. https://doi.org/10.1080/14719037.2019.1619810

Venturini T, Ricci D, Mauri M, Kimbell L, Meunier A (2015) Designing controversies and their publics. Des Issues 31(3):74–87. https://doi.org/10.1162/DESI_a_00340

Villa Alvarez DP, Auricchio V, Mortati M (2020) Design prototyping for policymaking. In: Boess S, Cheung M, Cain R (eds) Presented at the synergy—DRS International Conference 2020. https://doi.org/10.21606/drs.2020.271

Vink J, Koskela-Huotari K, Tronvoll B, Edvardsson B, Wetter-Edman K (2021) Service ecosystem design: propositions, process model, and future research agenda. J Serv Res 24(2):168–186. https://doi.org/10.1177/1094670520952537

Zimmerman J, Forlizzi J, Evenson S (2007) Research through design as a method for interaction design research in HCI. In: Proceedings of the SIGCHI conference on human factors in computing systems, ACM, New York, NY, USA, pp 493–502. https://doi.org/10.1145/1240624.1240704

**Open Access** This chapter is licensed under the terms of the Creative Commons Attribution 4.0 International License (http://creativecommons.org/licenses/by/4.0/), which permits use, sharing, adaptation, distribution and reproduction in any medium or format, as long as you give appropriate credit to the original author(s) and the source, provide a link to the Creative Commons license and indicate if changes were made.

The images or other third party material in this chapter are included in the chapter's Creative Commons license, unless indicated otherwise in a credit line to the material. If material is not included in the chapter's Creative Commons license and your intended use is not permitted by statutory regulation or exceeds the permitted use, you will need to obtain permission directly from the copyright holder.

# Chapter 5
# Design Thinking Practices for E-Participation

**Abstract** This chapter identifies design thinking practices for supporting e-participation. The chapter presents the five practices of (i) Meaning creation and sense-making, (ii) Publics formation, (iii) Co-production, (iv) Experimenting and prototyping, and (v) Changing organisational culture. Each of these practices is discussed against relevant case studies.

**Keywords** Design thinking practices · e-participation · Meaning-creation · Co-production · Organisational change · Publics formation · Prototyping

This chapter delves deeper into how DT practices can enhance e-participation, providing a detailed exploration of how each practice can foster public engagement. The analysis discusses the DT practices identified through the lens of the case studies introduced in Chapter 3. This approach not only illustrates the practical implementation of these practices but also highlights their effectiveness in fostering dynamic and more inclusive participation to the public discourse and public services.

## 5.1 Meaning Creation and Sense-Making: Valuing the Context and Communicating Better

The process of meaning creation and sense-making is core in DT and can significantly bolster e-participation. Since the early stages of the process, DT can aid public authorities in engaging citizens more effectively by offering methods and practices for (i) critical analysis of the context of operation (Dong and MacDonald 2017), (ii) user research to gain an in-depth understanding of local needs (Etches and Phetteplace 2013; Marsh 2018), and (iii) capturing factors that could influence the success or failure of new initiatives (Junginger 2014; Kimbell 2015; Lewis et al. 2020). Focusing on the context as an interplay of people, behaviours and environments can enhance e-participation by further orienting its activities. By rendering public issues (and their consequences) more tangible and specific, DT can enable people to participate as experts of a situation (e.g., the inhabitants of a neighbourhood) or process (e.g., school enrolling of children) (Dong and MacDonald 2017; Dorst 2011; Grönroos and Voima 2013), thereby empowering them to act as local innovators (Bogers et al. 2010).

Beyond meaning creation, DT's contribution regards supporting sense-making, such as clarifying public issues for enhancing citizen participation in the public discourse exploiting data visualisation (Al-Kodmany 2001; Alshuwaikhat and Nkwenti 2002). These techniques can help make sense of vast amounts of information by turning complex data into more graspable information, especially when designed to communicate information to citizens with varied levels of data literacy. Striking a balance between clarity and complexity (Venturini et al. 2015), data visualisation can support governments in informing about contextual conditions and disseminating insights to the public through clear and trustworthy representations. The provision of quality data which is made understandable has an undeniable role in favouring a more informed participation of citizens to the public discourse (Dimara et al. 2021). These dual, complementary perspectives concur to more effective information provision, which is pivotal in ensuring effective e-participation.

In this area, we can therefore say that DT's key contribution to e-participation lies in transforming the identification, perception, and framing of problems (Dorst 2011; Drews 2009; Mazé 2014). By putting people at the centre of the process, DT helps decision-makers mitigate individual cognitive biases (Liedtka 2015), fostering the development of more desirable services without neglecting governmental requirements.

### 5.1.1 #MyFrance2022

The #MyFrance2022 initiative is a relevant example of the transformative potential of e-participation in shaping the political discourse at national level, which embeds several DT principles. In terms of improving communication, several actions have been taken including an extensive digital engagement campaign, developed in collaboration with mainstream channels like France Bleu and France 3, and the platform make.org. This mobilised over one million French citizens in the lead-up to the presidential elections, and was conducive to framing and reframing political engagement. Rather than merely collecting opinions, the initiative reframed how electoral priorities are set by allowing citizens themselves to define and discuss what matters most to them. The result is a more granular understanding of local needs, capturing a broader spectrum of public opinions and nuancing local priorities in consideration of different demographic segments. This reimagining of the public's role in political discourse encouraged the exploration of novel perspectives on national priorities, directly affecting the framing of electoral debates.

Through the make.org platform, individuals are empowered to submit proposals and vote on future priorities, as a step ahead to make their voices integral to the shaping of the electoral agenda. In so doing, the initiative prioritised **human-centric**

**design** by involving citizens not just as participants, but as co-creators of the electoral agenda. This process is also **iterative and non-linear**, as it gathers relevant questions and opinions from citizens, and advances them to be included in the political debate.

The #MyFrance2022 initiative serves as a good example of meaning creation and sense-making within the context of e-participation. From the outset, the design of the campaign, characterised by targeted outreach efforts to various demographic groups, exemplifies the commitment to inclusivity. By reaching out to multiple target groups, the initiative fostered a participative environment that was adaptable and responsive to the needs of a broad spectrum of French society. This project effectively leveraged deliberative platforms to interpret and make sense of the complex, multi-layered, and sometimes ambiguous perspectives of a diverse citizenry. By providing a space where various viewpoints could be expressed, debated, and refined before being voiced, the initiative facilitated a deeper understanding of the public's concerns and aspirations.

The make.org platform plays a key role in the collection and synthesis of wide-ranging ideas and suggestions, favouring the transformation of abstract public sentiment into tangible electoral priorities. The dynamic interaction between the collection of proposals and subsequent public discussions exemplifies how meaning creation and sense-making can support unravelling complex public issues and translating them into actionable insights that form the groundwork of political agendas. It also enhanced the quality of the discourse ensuring that the final electoral priorities reflected a genuine consensus on what mattered most to the public.

## 5.2 Publics Formation: Engaging Publics Supporting Awareness and Plurality

The engagement of citizens in e-participation relies on more than their understanding of the issues at hand; the mere provision of clear information is not sufficient for effective action. To become experts, citizens need to be empowered to contribute to the public debate. Here, the practice of publics formation plays a pivotal role, associated with the generative influence that publics can exert (Le Dantec 2016). In e-participation, forming publics is key to create an environment conducive to constructive discourse and exchange, wherein expert publics can emerge as effective agents of change. Linked to this is also the concept of agonism which emphasises the inclusion of diversity of viewpoints, referred to as agonistic pluralism (Björgvinsson et al. 2012; DiSalvo 2010). Publics formation helps lay the groundwork for effective participation, fostering the creation of settings where to challenge the dominant views and rethink the norm of consensual decision-making processes in favour of tolerant debates among passionately engaged publics.

As such, DT's contribution lies in offering tools and methodologies that facilitate the formation of diverse publics and settings in which they can express themselves, ensuring the inclusion of multiple voices, and their chances to be heard and respected, thus making e-participation a more inclusive and representative process.

DT's emphasis on understanding different stakeholders' viewpoints strengthens the creation of a public that is not only well-informed but also active in shaping public priorities.

### 5.2.1 Better Reykjavik

Better Reykjavik is known as an online platform for empowering citizens to co-create ideas and co-produce solutions for urban improvements. By enabling residents to submit, discuss, and prioritise suggestions, from budget allocations to enhancements in public services, it is recognised to involve citizens while cultivating a sense of shared responsibility and ownership over urban development outcomes.

Despite the positive aspects of this case like the capability of engaging a statistically representative cross-section of Iceland's population, Better Reykjavik has encountered challenges in achieving true inclusiveness and representativeness, particularly concerning the participation of minority groups. This shortfall highlights a critical aspect of e-participation: the need for platforms to not only represent diverse demographics numerically but also to ensure that they are genuinely inclusive of the diverse makeup of the populace.

From a user-centred perspective, this platform would benefit from redesigning its interaction processes to better capture and integrate diverse viewpoints effectively, posing the concepts of agonism and pluralism at the core. Agonistic pluralism acknowledges the importance of incorporating diverse viewpoints, fostering environments where such perspectives can challenge dominant narratives and contribute to the discourse. This should go beyond seeking consensus; it should encourage debates that respect and value conflicting views as pivotal to democratic discourse. Adopting the practice of public formation, the initiative might enhance its capacity to form truly diverse publics, starting from a critical analysis of the context of operation and better including non- or under-represented groups. This process should start mapping the multiple stakeholders needed to represent the population and assessing their needs and expectations, facilitating the creation of settings where diverse publics can emerge as informed and influential participants.

Reconfiguring the interaction and participation mechanisms to promote wider and more equitable participation would not only result in reflecting a broader spectrum of societal voices but also in enriching the democratic process, emphasising the creation of solutions that are more representative and democratically legitimate.

### 5.2.2 Decidim Barcelona

Decidim has emerged as the flagship project of the Barcelona Digital City plan, representing a transformative approach to urban governance, digital commons, and citizens' rights, being considered a radical experiment in democracy that has gained international recognition. Originating from a robust partnership between technology activists and local councils, it is tailored to foster active civic participation, demonstrating how a digital platform can engage citizens in forming publics. Matter of factly, it leverages technology and caters to diverse participation needs while addressing critical aspects of inclusiveness and representation.

As such, this platform exemplifies a case of e-participation well aligned with DT principles, as it has an iterative, user-centred approach in the creation and continuous improvement of participatory processes.

Decidim's approach to publics formation is deeply rooted in its sociotechnological framework, which is designed to be open and adaptable, dedicated to continuous improvement and responsiveness to community needs. For instance, to address challenges such as digital literacy and engagement disparities, Decidim not only facilitates online democratic engagement but also actively promotes and supports physical meetings. This hybrid approach mitigates digital divide issues by enhancing the synergy between digital and conventional democratic processes, representing a committed response to the need for inclusivity. It ensures that all community members have the opportunity to participate effectively in the democratic process, regardless of their familiarity with digital tools.

Decidim provides a common space where individuals and groups can converge, spurring the formation of cohesive publics actively engaged in negotiating diverse viewpoints to foster generative discussions. Here, the social and material interdependencies within communities can be untangled and better understood. This process lays the groundwork for fostering a well-rounded, deeply informed public discourse, able to meet multiple and multi-level expectations and needs. The platform serves as a venue for mapping out interests and shared challenges and resources, thus enhancing collective problem-setting and subsequent problem-solving.

Finally, its design and operational principles are geared towards instilling and nurturing systemic change. By embedding authentic democratic engagement deeply into the operations of city governance, Decidim represents a cultural shift from traditional power dynamics, making governmental processes more transparent, accountable, and inclusive. This change goes beyond altering how decisions are made—it represents a transformation in how political and civic interactions are conceived and planned, fostering a culture of sustained participation and democratic innovation.

## 5.3 Co-production: From "Asking the Citizens" to "Co-producing with Citizens"

The shift from soliciting citizen feedback to actively co-producing with them represents a significant transformation in the management of public resources and the delivery of public services. This approach, underpinned by the concept of co-production, promises to enhance public participation (Durose and Richardson 2015; Liu 2021). Public sector innovation labs, such as living labs, fab labs, and policy labs, are serving as pioneering settings where this approach to co-production is being explored and refined (Deserti et al. 2022). Despite challenges are still evident (i.e., tensions due to the fact that citizen-proposed innovations clash with established public institutional practices), these labs are playing a crucial role in developing alternative ways to address public issues (Bentzen et al. 2020; Jukić et al. 2019; Linders 2012; Osborne et al. 2016), especially in addressing the high failure rates often seen in user experience (Khan and Krishnan 2021).

The engagement models employed by these labs could be highly relevant to e-participation. They offer a framework to integrate multiple types of knowledge while transcending traditional interests and representation mechanisms. A further direction for improvement in this area is the definition of a systematic approach to value creation that underscores the interaction between e-participation procedures and the broader societal context (Strokosch and Osborne 2020). In this process, DT can provide support by temporarily flattening hierarchical structures and fostering an inclusive environment for exploring ideas and their consequences.

### 5.3.1 Go Vocal, Former CitizenLab

The use of CitizenLab, now Go Vocal platform, for the redevelopment of Kapermolen Park in Hasselt, Belgium, exemplifies a co-creation process infused with co-production where citizens are enabled to actively and effectively contribute to urban planning decisions. Beyond allowing co-creation of ideas, the novelty resides in co-producing solutions to foster a sense of fairness and trust within the community. This can also bolster a sense of ownership, strengthening the accountability and legitimacy of the resulting projects. However, it implies consistent efforts in rethinking processes and tools to include iterative refinement of initiatives through community feedback and ongoing dialogue, aiming at ensuring that final outcomes are closely aligned with community needs.

In the specific case of Hasselt, the e-participation platform supported the city in collecting and analysing a rich dataset of ideas and feedback, nurturing a design-driven and data-informed approach that accurately reflected the community's true needs and desires. Beyond the democratisation provided by the co-creation approach, the co-production aspects involved have enhanced the integration of these inputs into the actual planning of city projects, ensuring that residents felt involved and valued in the decision-making.

Within e-participation platforms, co-production goes beyond simply gathering feedback; it means actively involving stakeholders in the design and progressive implementation of the solution. This engagement ensures that citizens are not merely passive recipients of services or decisions, but active contributors that can shape them. This openness also allows citizens to directly deal with issues, thereby enabling them to provide more pertinent and impactful feedback. Engaging users in co-production offers valuable insights that span from usability to improvement of service journeys, sometimes aiding in the design of more intuitive solutions.

Ultimately, the integration of more tangible activities in a public participation process can significantly enhance the effectiveness of outcomes. Living labs, fab labs, and policy labs represent ideal settings for hosting these types of actions, where multiple stakeholders—including citizens, government officials, and experts—can collaborate more dynamically. In these labs, stakeholders engage and break down the usual barriers of more formal settings. Moreover, the physical presence in labs encourages a more empathetic and connected approach to common understanding and decision-making, which is often lost in purely digital interactions.

## 5.4 Experimenting and Prototyping: Bridging the Gap Between Ideas and Practical Applications

Prototyping in digital public services allows experimentation of new solutions by engaging citizens in real but controlled environments. This approach enables the testing of new ideas while minimising innovation risks, as it allows for comparing the performance of prototypes against expectations. In e-participation, prototyping could involve piloting new forms of e-consultations, crowd-sourcing initiatives, or online forums for policy dialogues, helping understand which topics or approaches better resonate with the public and how they affect participation quality and outcomes. Experimentation can also include the use of gamification (Agbozo and Chepurov 2018; Hassan and Hamari 2020), scenarios, or storytelling techniques (Couldry 2008; Dzida and Freitag 1998) to make the participation process more engaging and to gather richer, more nuanced insights and inputs from participants for service designing, policy-making and possibly improving governance at large.

One significant advantage of experimenting with prototypes is the ability to encounter and learn from low-impact failures at early stages, while exploiting them as boundary objects able to trigger organisational learning (Coughlan et al. 2007; del Olmo and Morelli 2022). Prototypes are not just triggers for learning but also potent tools for knowledge exchange (Bogers and Horst 2014; Coughlan et al. 2007). They can facilitate interaction and collaboration between citizens and public officials on specific challenges, helping to establish a shared understanding and constructively acknowledging differences. In the process of prototyping, the interplay of multiple actors can lead to the breakdown of functional, hierarchical, and organisational barriers, leading to improved dialogue and collaboration (Bogers and Horst 2014). This dynamic can make the e-participation process more inclusive and open, ultimately contributing to the development of solutions that are collectively owned and better suited for implementation.

DT can thus strengthen e-participation through prototyping incorporating user-centricity and iterative development. These principles ensure that the prototypes developed are not only technically sound but also resonate with the actual needs and preferences of the users. This alignment might increase the likelihood of successful adoption and effective implementation of the proposed digital public services, making the e-participation process more robust, user-friendly, and impactful.

### 5.4.1 Decide Madrid

Decide Madrid was used in 2020 to launch a comprehensive participatory process as part of the city's renaturalization strategy.[1] This aimed to gather detailed information about the specific needs of the neighbourhoods and districts of Madrid while channelling citizen initiatives that could be implemented and enabling contact with individuals who could contribute to the development of the strategy. Decide Madrid helped conduct a survey to deepen understanding of the public's perceptions and concerns related to health, environment, and urban issues. This sparked a participatory process that empowered citizens to actively design urban spaces using a 3D planning tool (also made available through Decide Madrid), allowing them to propose and discuss potential uses and activities for these areas. The initiative saw significant engagement, with 344 plots receiving a total of 623 proposals uploaded by participants. Additionally, technical workshops were organised to debate nature-based solutions for cities. These sessions brought together diverse and complementary knowledge from experts, scientists, and people to reason on multi-actor partnerships, thereby creating a collective project and fostering community learning.

Overall, the process allowed for continuous refinement of proposals through active citizen participation, embodying a true prototyping process. The iterative feedback loops, where proposals are refined based on public and technical input before final voting, illustrate a dynamic prototyping environment where each stage of the process serves as a test bed for new ideas and methods, with continuous improvements informed by user interactions and technical assessments. Further, the platform provides updates as projects are implemented, enhancing transparency and trust. This approach to public engagement exemplifies a radical experiment in democratic innovation and urban governance, reflecting the need for a significant shift in how cities interact with their citizens.

## 5.5 Changing Organisational Culture: Favouring Knowledge Transfer and Capacity Building

Integrating DT into e-participation requires a focus on learning-by-doing and a commitment to experimentation and change. This should be complemented with reflective practices capable of ensuring sustainable transformation, including the transfer and retention of knowledge within public institutions (Payne et al. 2008). Through e-participation, citizens can increasingly contribute to public value creation,

---

[1] https://estrategiaurbana.madrid.es/wp-content/uploads/2020/06/Isla-de-Color.pdf.

being engaged on matters related to public service development and delivery, policy-making, and wider public issues. From an institutional perspective, the learning that comes from such practices also needs to be retained and enacted, for instance by raising awareness about the benefits and advantages of novel participatory approaches that might feed into reflexivity (Beckman and Barry 2007; Geraldi and Söderlund 2016). The same learning can also encourage the revision of existing policies, practices, and procedures, thus transforming institutional culture to become more inclusive and responsive to citizens' needs.

DT can play a key role in transforming how e-participation is conceived and institutionalised by public administrations, encouraging continuous improvement and collaboration based on user-centricity principles. Embracing such a mindset implies overcoming traditional processes towards adopting new ways of thinking and doing, that are grounded on principles of adaptability, innovation, and openness.

### 5.5.1 vTaiwan

The consultation process vTaiwan exemplifies how learning-by-doing and a commitment to experimentation and change can be integrated in e-participation processes, fundamentally transforming organisational culture within public institutions. Originated as a collaboration between the government and g0v volunteers, vTaiwan operates as a neutral mediator in Taiwanese politics, being widely recognised for its legitimacy, effectiveness, and credibility. It actively convenes a diverse array of stakeholders, utilising a combination of online platforms and offline events to facilitate a process aimed at achieving a 'rough consensus' among participants on specific policy issues, often controversial. The initiative recently started making use of the Pol.is tool to go beyond traditional comment-reply structures, reducing trolling and creating visual maps of consensus rather than division, in a constructive dialogue environment.

Nevertheless, the impact of vTaiwan on Taiwan's institutional democratic capacity is broader and deeper. In the first instance, the platform facilitates frequent interactions between the government and the public, where rapid responses enhance transparency and accountability and help bridge the gap between public input and policy outcome. Its dynamic interactions, however, foster more than responsive governance; they cultivate a learning-oriented culture within public institutions. For instance, the push towards uptaking and experimenting with proposals coming from the society promotes an organisational attitude of continuous improvement and user-centricity, making the e-participation process more robust and impactful.

Despite its successes, vTaiwan also faces significant challenges that underscore the importance of maintaining independence and transparency to sustain public trust. The government's veto power over discussion topics and the non-binding nature of vTaiwan's recommendations could undermine its perceived autonomy and effectiveness. Furthermore, attracting new users remains a challenge; despite its innovative approach, the platform has engaged only a fraction of Taiwan's population. This is compounded by the reliance on volunteers for its operation, which poses limitations on scalability and continuous engagement.

The initiative is particularly relevant in terms of knowledge transfer and capacity building. It benefits from substantial government buy-in, which was initially fostered by the minister Tsai Ing-wen who served as the 7th president of Taiwan from 2016 to 2024, showing consistent commitment to hosting offline meetings in government buildings and ensuring that all government ministries maintain active engagement on the vTaiwan forum. This setup mandates that any public inquiry regarding laws or regulations must be addressed by the relevant ministry within seven days on the forum, facilitating an open and responsive communication channel between citizens and government. Additionally, the robust support of volunteers plays a crucial role in sustaining the vTaiwan process, which involves multiple, resource-intensive stages. Volunteers assist not only in moderating online discussions and transcribing offline meetings but also in performing various administrative tasks. This volunteer support ensures the smooth operation of the platform and the effective compilation and summarisation of citizen contributions, which deeply support informed decision-making.

vTaiwan operates with a high degree of agility and independence, which allows for a flexible and experimental participatory approach. This is characterised by the use of open-source software and a toolkit that is continuously updated and improved by a community of designers and developers. Such an agile operation enables vTaiwan to adapt swiftly to the evolving demands of public engagement and technological innovation. Moreover, the collaborative nature of vTaiwan, involving representatives from multiple or all political parties, increases the likelihood that the outcomes of the consultation process will be respected and acted upon. This cross-party support during the consultation phase means that no party typically wants to block the progress of proposals, leading to a higher rate of legislative success. This dynamic not only fosters a culture of consensus but also ensures that elected officials take full responsibility for their decisions, knowing they reflect the popular consensus and are backed by a comprehensive understanding of public sentiment and factual underpinnings.

The structured feedback mechanism within vTaiwan, which requires ministries to respond to public inquiries within a set timeframe, has institutionalised a culture of responsiveness and accountability. This practice not only streamlines the flow of information but also builds trust and enhances transparency between the government and its citizens. As ministries engage more directly with citizen queries and concerns, they gain a deeper understanding of public sentiment and of the societal implications of their policies, which in turn informs and refines their regulatory and legislative frameworks. From an institutional perspective, the continuous learning deriving from the initiative keeps enriching the understanding within government bodies of the practical benefits and strategic advantages of more participatory and inclusive approaches to governance. Further, this awareness nurtures institutional reflexivity by encouraging public institutions to continuously assess and adapt their methods and policies to respond to direct citizen feedback and engagement.

Overall, this model not only empowers citizens to actively participate in the democratic process but also equips government officials with relevant insights and feedback for making more informed and attuned decisions, resulting in better alignment with public interests. As such, vTaiwan stands as a transformative force in civic engagement, leveraging a fertile institutional ground to further instil inclusive and collaborative practices in how policy-making is conceived and executed.

### 5.5.2  Scottish's "We Asked, You Said, We Did"

The "We asked, you said, we did" is recognised as instrumental in establishing a culture of consultation within the Scottish Government. It operates across various stages of the policy cycle—from policy analysis and preparation to implementation—ensuring that public feedback is not only solicited but meaningfully incorporated into decision-making. The initiative is rooted in **experimentation in real contexts,** with the government engaging directly with real-world public feedback mechanisms, compelling it to challenge and adapt its established norms and practices. The comprehensive integration of public inputs signifies a high commitment to inclusive governance and increases the accountability of policymakers. The initiative significantly impacts the organisation's practices by requiring it to conclude each consultation phase with a detailed report that articulates public feedback and the government's subsequent actions. By institutionalising such a feedback mechanism, the Scottish Government demonstrates a systemic shift toward greater transparency and accountability. The publication of detailed outcomes helps demystify government actions for the public, bridging the gap between citizen input and governmental action. This level of documentation and responsiveness requires effort and resource allocation, but contributes in maintaining public trust and showing tangible outcomes of public input. Moreover, this approach signifies a systemic change in how the government interacts with its citizens, moving beyond superficial engagement to a robust, responsive model where public input is visibly integrated into policymaking and service delivery. The transparency provided by continuous reporting offers citizens with visible proof that their contributions have a direct impact on policy outcomes, thereby enhancing their trust in the consultation process.

This approach represents a systemic change in how the government interacts with its citizens. It moves beyond tokenistic engagement to a more robust, responsive model where public input is not only solicited but also visibly integrated into policymaking and service delivery. Additionally, the initiative's structured feedback and reporting mechanism embody an **iterative and non-linear process**. Each phase of consultation and the subsequent integration of feedback into policy-making are not seen as final but as steps in an ongoing cycle of refinement and evolution. This adaptive process highlights a departure from traditional, linear approaches to policy development, fostering a governmental culture that values flexibility, continual learning, and responsiveness.

However, the initiative also points out the need for improvements in how consultations are designed and conducted, particularly in addressing challenges such as the framing of questions and the genuine integration of diverse viewpoints. The inconsistency in how feedback is embodied and operationalised across different government departments indicates a need for more uniform practices and a deeper commitment to stakeholder engagement. Addressing these issues may involve targeted training for policy teams, improving the design of consultation questions, and fostering a stronger commitment to integrating stakeholder feedback.

**Funding** Some of the reasoning presented in this work derive from knowledge and insights from the project "AI4GOV, Artificial Intelligence for Public Services", Action No. 2020-EU-IA-0064, co-financed by the EU CEF Telecom (No. INEA/CEF/ICT/A2020/2265375) [ai4gov-hub.eu; ai4 gov-master.eu]. The opinions expressed herewith are solely of the authors and do not necessarily reflect the point of view of any EU institution.

# References

Agbozo E, Chepurov E (2018) Enhancing e-participation via gamification of e-government platforms: a possible solution to SubSaharan African e-government initiatives. In: CEUR workshop proceedings, vol 2145, pp 83–86 CEUR-WS. https://ceur-ws.org/Vol-2145/p14.pdf

Al-Kodmany K (2001) Visualization tools and methods for participatory planning and design. J Urban Technol 8(2):1–37. https://doi.org/10.1080/106307301316904772

Alshuwaikhat HM, Nkwenti DI (2002) Visualizing decisionmaking: perspectives on collaborative and participative approach to sustainable urban planning and management. Environ Plan B: Plan Des 29(4):513–531. https://doi.org/10.1068/b12818

Beckman SL, Barry M (2007) Innovation as a learning process: embedding design thinking. Calif Manage Rev 50(1):25–56. https://doi.org/10.2307/41166415

Bentzen TØ, Sørensen E, Torfing J (2020) Strengthening public service production, administrative problem solving, and political leadership through co-creation of innovative public value outcomes. Innov J: Public Sect Innov J 25(1):1–28

Björgvinsson E, Ehn P, Hillgren P-A (2012) Agonistic participatory design: working with marginalised social movements. CoDesign 8(2–3):127–144. https://doi.org/10.1080/15710882.2012.672577

Bogers M, Afuah A, Bastian B (2010) Users as innovators: a review, critique, and future research directions. J Manag 36(4):857–875. https://doi.org/10.1177/0149206309353944

Bogers M, Horst W (2014) Collaborative prototyping: cross-fertilization of knowledge in prototype-driven problem solving. J Prod Innov Manag 31(4):744–764. https://doi.org/10.1111/jpim.12121

Coughlan P, Suri JF, Canales K (2007) Prototypes as (design) tools for behavioral and organizational change: a design-based approach to help organizations change work behaviors. J Appl Behav Sci 43(1):122–134. https://doi.org/10.1177/0021886306297722

Couldry N (2008) Digital storytelling, media research and democracy: Conceptual choices and alternative futures. In: Digital storytelling, mediatized stories: self-representations in new media, pp 41–60

del Olmo MV, Morelli N (2022) Service journeys as boundary objects in participatory processes for multi-stakeholder engagement: the case of the easyrights journeys. In: Lockton D, Lenzi S, Hekkert P, Oak A, Sádaba J, Lloyd P (Eds,) DRS 2022. Design Research Society. https://doi.org/10.21606/drs.2022.539

# References

Deserti A, Real M, Schmittinger F (2022) Co-creation for responsible research and innovation: experimenting with design methods and tools. Springer Nature. https://doi.org/10.1007/978-3-030-78733-2

Dimara E, Zhang H, Tory M, Franconeri S (2021) The unmet data visualization needs of decision makers within organizations. IEEE Trans Visual Comput Graphics 28(12):4101–4112. https://doi.org/10.1109/TVCG.2021.3074023

DiSalvo C (2010) Design, democracy and agonistic pluralism. In: DRS2010 research papers. Presented at the DRS2010: design and complexity, Montreal, Canada. https://dl.designresearchsociety.org/drs-conference-papers/drs2010/researchpapers/31

Dong A, MacDonald E (2017) From observations to insights: the hilly road to value creation. In: Analysing design thinking: studies of cross-cultural co-creation. CRC Press, London, UK, pp 465–482

Dorst K (2011) The core of 'design thinking' and its application. Interpret Des Think 32(6):521–532. https://doi.org/10.1016/j.destud.2011.07.006

Drews C (2009) Unleashing the full potential of design thinking as a business method. Des Manag Rev 20(3):38–44. https://doi.org/10.1111/j.1948-7169.2009.00020.x

Durose C, Richardson L (2015) Designing public policy for co-production: theory, practice and change. Policy Press, Bristol, UK. https://doi.org/10.2307/j.ctt1t896qg

Dzida W, Freitag R (1998) Making use of scenarios for validating analysis and design. IEEE Trans Softw Eng 24(12):1182–1196

Etches A, Phetteplace E (2013) Know thy users: user research techniques to build empathy and improve decision-making. Ref User Serv Q 53(1):13–17. http://www.jstor.org/stable/refuseserq.53.1.13. Accessed 13 Jan 2024

Geraldi J, Söderlund J (2016) Project studies and engaged scholarship: directions towards contextualized and reflexive research on projects. Int J Manag Proj Bus 9(4):767–797. https://doi.org/10.1108/IJMPB-02-2016-0016

Grönroos C, Voima P (2013) Critical service logic: making sense of value creation and co-creation. J Acad Mark Sci 41(2):133–150. https://doi.org/10.1007/s11747-012-0308-3

Hassan L, Hamari J (2020) Gameful civic engagement: a review of the literature on gamification of e-participation. Gov Inf Q 37(3):101461. https://doi.org/10.1016/j.giq.2020.101461

Jukić T, Pevcin P, Benčina J, Dečman M, Vrbek S (2019) Collaborative innovation in public administration: theoretical background and research trends of co-production and co-creation. Adm Sci 9(4). https://doi.org/10.3390/admsci9040090

Junginger S (2014) Towards policy-making as designing: policy-making beyond problem-solving and decision-making. In: Bason C (ed) Design for policy. Routledge, London, UK, pp 57–69. https://doi.org/10.4324/9781315576640

Khan A, Krishnan S (2021) Citizen engagement in co-creation of e-government services: a process theory view from a meta-synthesis approach. Internet Res 31(4):1318–1375. https://doi.org/10.1108/INTR-03-2020-0116

Kimbell L (2015) Applying design approaches to policy making: discovering policy lab. University of Brighton, Brighton, UK

Le Dantec CA (2016) Designing publics. MIT Press, Cambridge, MA

Lewis JM, McGann M, Blomkamp E (2020) When design meets power: design thinking, public sector innovation and the politics of policymaking. Policy Polit 48(1):111–130. https://doi.org/10.1332/030557319X15579230420081

Liedtka J (2015) Perspective: linking design thinking with innovation outcomes through cognitive bias reduction. J Prod Innov Manag 32(6):925–938. https://doi.org/10.1111/jpim.12163

Linders D (2012) From e-government to we-government: defining a typology for citizen coproduction in the age of social media. In: Social media in government—selections from the 12th annual international conference on digital government research (dg.o2011), vol 29, no 4, pp 446–454. https://doi.org/10.1016/j.giq.2012.06.003

Liu HK (2021) Crowdsourcing: citizens as coproducers of public services. Policy Internet 13(2):315–331. https://doi.org/10.1002/poi3.249

Marsh, S. (2018). User research: a practical guide to designing better products and services. Kogan Page Publishers, London, UK/New York, NY

Mazé R (2014) Our common future? Political questions for designing social innovation. In: Lim Y, Niedderer K, Redström J, Stolterman E, Valtonen A (eds) Proceedings of DRS2014 international conference. Design's big debates. Presented at the design's big debates—DRS international conference 2014. Design Research Society, Umeå, Sweden. https://dl.designresearchsociety.org/drs-conference-papers/drs2014/researchpapers/41/

Osborne SP, Radnor Z, Strokosch K (2016) Co-production and the co-creation of value in public services: a suitable case for treatment? Public Manag Rev 18(5):639–653. https://doi.org/10.1080/14719037.2015.1111927

Payne AF, Storbacka K, Frow P (2008) Managing the co-creation of value. J Acad Mark Sci 36(1):83–96. https://doi.org/10.1007/s11747-007-0070-0

Strokosch K, Osborne SP (2020) Co-experience, co-production and co-governance: an ecosystem approach to the analysis of value creation. Policy Polit 48(3):425–442. https://doi.org/10.1332/030557320X15857337955214

Venturini T, Ricci D, Mauri M, Kimbell L, Meunier A (2015) Designing controversies and their publics. Des Issues 31(3):74–87. https://doi.org/10.1162/DESI_a_00340

**Open Access** This chapter is licensed under the terms of the Creative Commons Attribution 4.0 International License (http://creativecommons.org/licenses/by/4.0/), which permits use, sharing, adaptation, distribution and reproduction in any medium or format, as long as you give appropriate credit to the original author(s) and the source, provide a link to the Creative Commons license and indicate if changes were made.

The images or other third party material in this chapter are included in the chapter's Creative Commons license, unless indicated otherwise in a credit line to the material. If material is not included in the chapter's Creative Commons license and your intended use is not permitted by statutory regulation or exceeds the permitted use, you will need to obtain permission directly from the copyright holder.

# Chapter 6
# Addressing E-Participation Barriers with Design Thinking

**Abstract** This chapter examines the application of design thinking in enhancing e-participation by aligning DT practices with identified barriers to participation. The chapter discusses practical strategies for leveraging DT to address issues such as digital illiteracy and lack of engagement, providing a framework for implementing more effective and inclusive e-participation initiatives.

**Keywords** Design thinking · E-Participation · Framework · Public engagement · Barrier mitigation

## 6.1 E-Participation Barriers Against DT Practices

In their systematic review (Oliveira and Garcia 2019), explored the factors contributing to limited citizen participation, categorising these obstacles into technical and non-technical barriers. Technical barriers pertain to issues that can be resolved through adjustments or enhancements in information and communication technology (ICT). Differently, non-technical barriers concern a broader range of impediments not directly linked to technological solutions. These barriers, while independent, can interact and potentially exacerbate each other. For instance, a misalignment between the topics discussed and citizens' everyday concerns might lead to a disinterest in political matters. Addressing one barrier might inadvertently mitigate another, such as fostering political engagement by encouraging participation in online discussions.

Figure 6.1 elaborates on (Oliveira and Garcia's 2019) classification of 15 e-participation barriers according to their severity. Technical barriers are coded in black and with a circle symbol while non-technical ones are grey and anticipated by a triangle. At the base of the pyramid are foundational barriers that are relatively easier to address, while the top of the pyramid features the most complex barriers that require significant structural efforts to overcome. This arrangement highlights the varying degrees of difficulty to face in addressing these issues, from straightforward solutions like improving accessibility to e-participation tools, to more challenging tasks such as integrating e-participation systems within existing governmental frameworks.

Technical barriers often offer clearer pathways for resolution through technological interventions, such as improving accessibility or enhancing internet and IT infrastructure. In contrast, non-technical barriers often hinge on changing public attitudes and behaviours, such as combating digital illiteracy, promoting awareness of participation opportunities, and ensuring governmental transparency. These challenges are not easily overcome by government actions alone but require a holistic approach involving continuous education and updates to government websites to maintain relevance and ease of access. Complex issues like political disengagement, passive user behaviour, and the need for content creation by a broader user

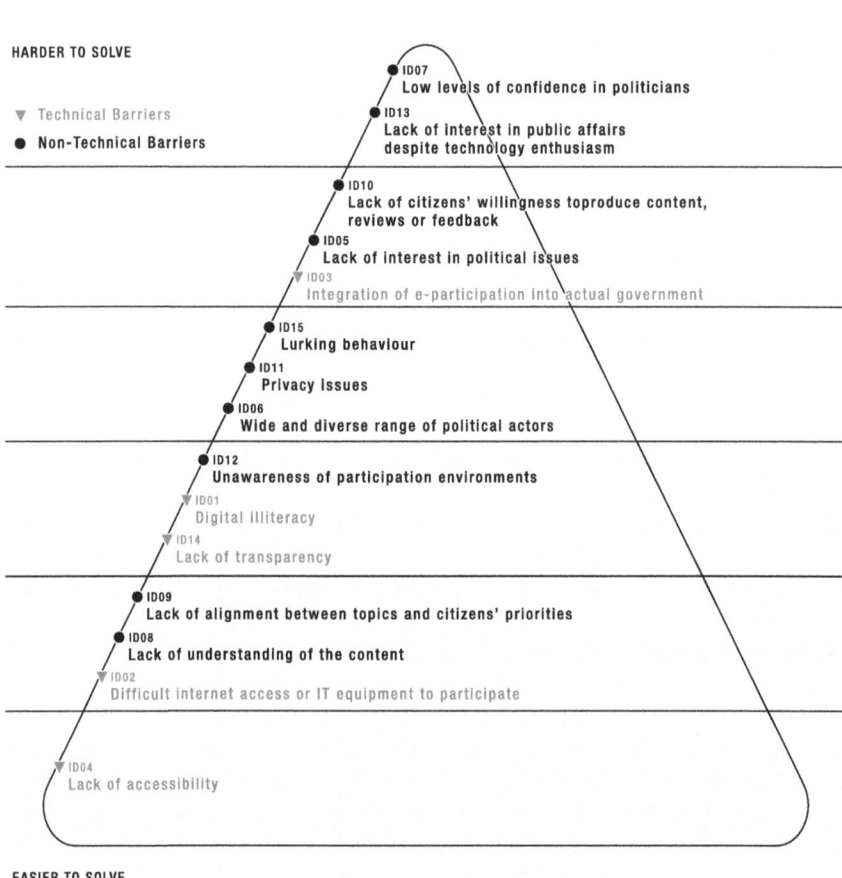

**Fig. 6.1** Barrier's degree of severity, adapted from (Oliveira and Garcia 2019)

## 6.1 E-Participation Barriers Against DT Practices

base involve more profound changes in government strategy and public engagement practices. Moreover, maintaining data privacy and securing government platforms against fraud are pivotal, demanding robust protective measures to ensure safe and trustworthy e-participation environments.

In Fig. 6.2, the 15 e-participation barriers are cross-referenced with DT practices, thereby framing an analysis of how DT can potentially mitigate issues in e-participation. Each barrier is matched with one or more DT practices that can help address it, offering a structured approach to understanding and potentially overcoming these challenges. The process through which the matching was performed builds on literature (see Table 4.2) to infer the potential of DT practices to nurture and transform e-participation. Inferences have been created through iterative discussions among expert researchers, which tended to couple each barrier with at least one DT practice. However, it is important to acknowledge that some barriers, such as "Difficult internet access or IT equipment to participate" (ID02), are mostly infrastructural. Here, DT practices tend to be mostly "cosmetic" and superficial. Addressing these types of barriers necessitates a more systemic approach that extends beyond the scope of DT, involving comprehensive policy and infrastructure development to ensure equitable access and participation.

The e-participation barriers identified by Oliveira and Garcia are below summarised following the original grouping into technical and non-technical categories, pointing out the issues inhibiting citizen engagement and participation in electronic government platforms.

**Technical barriers** include digital illiteracy, where a significant portion of the population, especially the elderly and those generally averse to technology, lack the necessary skills to utilise ICTs. This limitation often restricts their access to and engagement with digital platforms. To address this, it is often suggested to adopt more familiar platforms like X or messaging systems like WhatsApp to increase engagement. Additionally, access issues persist as some individuals, particularly in lower-income groups, still lack necessary internet or computing resources despite high smartphone penetration in many regions. The recommendation here involves integrating online and offline participation channels. Additionally, e-participation tools should be accessible to all, spanning from those with disabilities and impairments. Another significant technical barrier is the lack of transparency in government e-participation initiatives, which can diminish trust and reduce citizen participation. This barrier is characterised by a perceived lack of openness and two-way communication, and addressing it involves enhancing transparency and maintaining updated, accessible data. Furthermore, many e-participation initiatives remain at the pilot stage and are not fully integrated into governmental processes and implemented, limiting their scale and impact while reducing reliability of the governmental institution that organised the initiative. Successful integration requires adapting to social complexities, political culture, organisational structures, and technological dependencies.

**Non-technical barriers** concern a range of social and psychological factors that deter engagement. A general lack of interest in politics, particularly among young people and those who do not see direct relevance to their daily lives, poses a significant

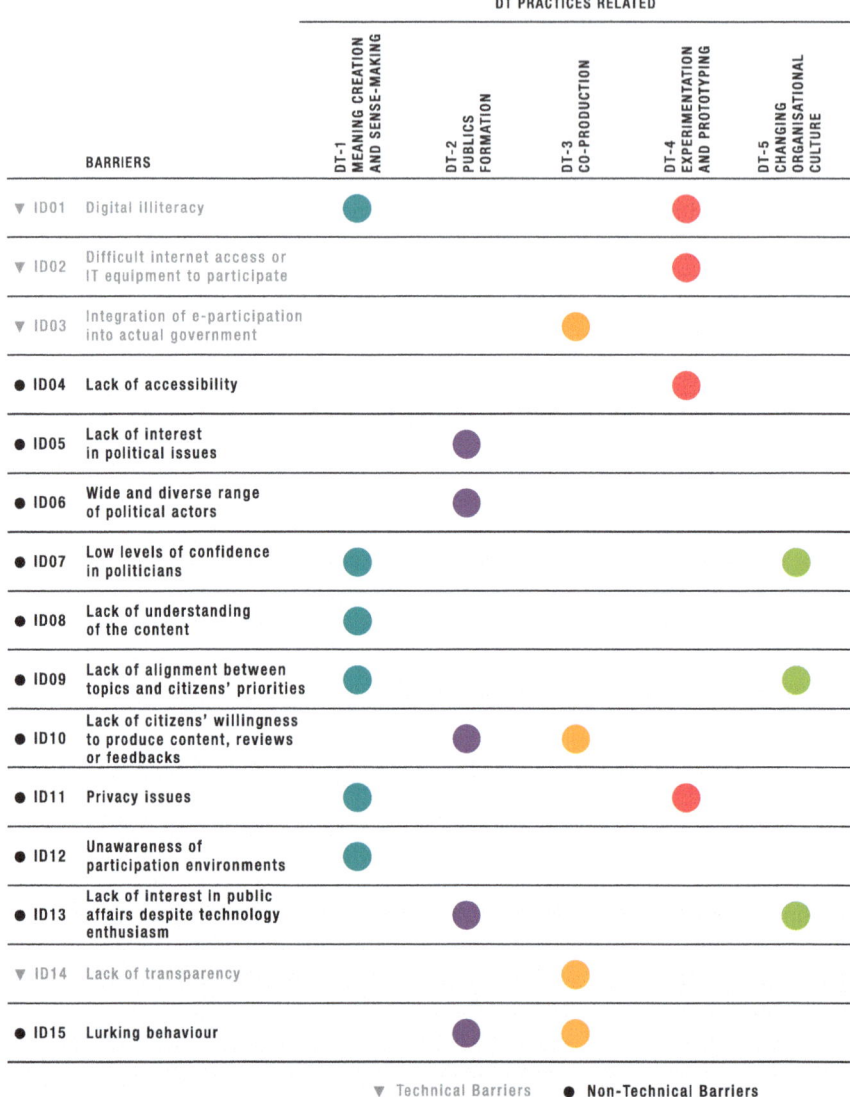

**Fig. 6.2** The 15 e-participation barriers cross-referenced with DT practices

challenge. Governments are encouraged to meet citizens where they are, rather than expecting them to initiate engagement. Political scepticism about citizens' capacity to contribute meaningfully to government decisions is prevalent among politicians who may view public engagement merely as a formality rather than a substantive contribution to governance. The presence of diverse political actors with differing agendas can also hinder effective e-participation, as some may view public engagement as an

## 6.1 E-Participation Barriers Against DT Practices

imposition rather than a valuable contribution. Privacy concerns, particularly in light of widespread privacy issues and scandals, may make citizens reluctant to engage with governmental platforms that require personal information, fearing misuse. Moreover, citizens often struggle with understanding government documents due to their complexity and technical language, which can discourage participation. If the topics discussed on e-participation platforms do not align with the everyday concerns of citizens, their engagement is likely to be minimal, making the relevance of topics crucial. Many users prefer to consume content rather than create it, presenting a challenge in generating active participation and feedback on e-participation platforms. Lack of awareness about e-participation platforms due to insufficient promotion and the slow pace of dissemination is a significant barrier. Some users may be drawn to the novelty of technology rather than a genuine interest in public affairs, leading to shallow engagement. Finally, the phenomenon of lurking, where users benefit from others' contributions without actively participating themselves, can undermine the collective efficacy of e-participation efforts.

The following paragraphs present a comprehensive alignment of DT practices with such identified barriers, offering insights into how the first can be strategically adopted to enhance the effectiveness of e-participation platforms and initiatives (Table 6.1).

DT-1 enhances e-participation by leveraging on deeply understanding user needs and framing contextual issues effectively. Considering the barriers to effective e-participation, this approach can help address digital literacy (ID01) by informing the design of more intuitive interfaces and user journeys, simplifying interactions, and fostering deeper engagement with content itself. Additionally, DT-1 can also aid in translating complex policy language and digital interactions into forms that are more comprehensible to the general public (ID08), thus demystifying content filled with bureaucratic jargon, empowering people with the possibility of contributing to the discourse. It can also serve to enhance transparency in e-participation processes, clarifying why citizens' opinions are relevant and how outputs are considered by politicians, in the direction of improved two-way communication between governments and citizens (ID07 and ID12). As such, DT-1 can help align government initiatives with the actual needs and priorities of the society, ensuring that e-participation initiatives reflect and respond to public concerns more effectively (ID09). Moreover, online interactions may also introduce significant privacy and data protection risks, especially as users may unknowingly disclose personal data or reveal sensitive information including personal beliefs and political opinions (ID11). These interactions often occur on platforms that use third-party applications, making these third parties the data controllers. DT-1 can help grasp a deeper understanding of users' perceptions of data usage in such environments, identifying strategies to answer concerns and risks associated with the sharing of their data. Such insights can be guided by design-driven approaches to improve how privacy measures and data protection policies are communicated, ultimately enhancing transparency and building trust in e-participation (Table 6.2).

**Table. 6.1** Alignment of "DT-1: Meaning creation and sense-making" with e-participation barriers

| DT practice | ID | Barrier related | Needs | How DT can support e-participation |
|---|---|---|---|---|
| DT-1: Meaning creation and sense-making | ID01 | Digital illiteracy | Simplification of interfaces; making technology more intuitive | Design intuitive interfaces<br>Simplify complex processes<br>Improve platforms accessibility |
| | ID07 | Low levels of confidence in politicians | Developing strategies for transparency and effective communication | Strategies to enhance transparency<br>Improve communication between politicians/governments and citizens |
| | ID08 | Lack of understanding of the content (unclear language) | Translating complex content into understandable language | Make complex content more graspable and comprehensible |
| | ID09 | Lack of alignment between the topics being discussed and the daily issues and priorities of the citizen | Facilitating better alignment of government initiatives with citizen needs | Enhance alignment with what truly matters to the public<br>Identify insights as drivers for decision-making |
| | ID11 | Privacy issues | Enhancing communication of privacy measures and data protection policies | Understand citizens' concerns<br>Develop strategies for better communicating how concerns are addressed<br>Clarify data usage and processing |
| | ID12 | Unawareness of participation environments | Creating meaningful awareness campaigns | Highlight benefits of e-participation<br>Show the impact of e-participation initiatives on decision-making processes<br>Outline the real value of e-participation for citizens |

6.1 E-Participation Barriers Against DT Practices

**Table. 6.2** Alignment of "DT-2: Publics formation" with e-participation barriers

| DT practice | ID | Barrier related | Needs | How DT can support e-participation |
|---|---|---|---|---|
| DT-2: Publics formation | ID05 | Lack of interest in political issues | Making e-participation more engaging and relevant to citizens | Better address citizen's interests and expectations<br>Make e-participation relevant for wider audiences |
| | ID06 | Wide and diverse range of political actors | Incorporating diverse political inputs constructively | Support the inclusion of diverse political perspectives<br>Make e-participation representative of multiple viewpoints |
| | ID10 | Lack of citizens' willingness to produce content, reviews or feedbacks | Encouraging collaboration and inclusiveness in participation | Design engagement strategies for more inclusive e-participation processes<br>Share outcomes to show the relevance of citizens' contribution |
| | ID13 | Lack of interest in public affairs although enthusiasm for new technology | Leveraging tech interest and familiarity to foster civic engagement | Leverage the potential of technology as a trigger for wider engagement |
| | ID15 | Lurking behaviour | Motivating passive users to become active participants | Design collaborative environments where passive users are motivated to contribute actively |

DT-2 focuses on directly leveraging the diversity of citizen interests, perspectives, and knowledge. This practice specifically addresses the challenge of political disengagement (ID05) by making e-participation initiatives and platforms more relevant to a broader audience. It aids more tailored interactions to better meet the varied interests, expertises, and expectations of citizens. In environments characterised by a wide range of political actors with their own interest and power dynamics (ID06), DT-2 can support designing a strategic inclusion of diverse political perspectives. This ensures that e-participation initiatives are truly representative of multiple political perspectives.

Additionally, DT-2 tackles the issue of citizens' reluctance to produce content, conduct reviews, or provide feedback (ID10) by encouraging the design of strategies able to better explain the relevance of their engagement. Strategies can be put in place to involve people with specific knowledge and know-hows as expert publics. Public formation would allow them to become effective agents of change, being empowered to challenge the dominant views. These strategies should also invite to more consistently share the outcomes of the process, demonstrating the tangible impact of citizens' contributions to decision-making. In this sense, DT-2 also addresses the challenge of lurking behaviour (ID15) by encouraging the design of more collaborative environments able to stimulate and inspire passive users to become active contributors. These environments should not only provide platforms for interaction but favourable settings which foster a sense of community and shared purpose. DT-2 can significantly contribute to increasing dynamicity and inclusiveness of deliberation, in a fruitful logic of agonistic pluralism that capitalises citizens' expertise to improve the public debate.

Finally, from a different perspective, in situations where there is an enthusiasm for technology but a corresponding lack of interest in public affairs (ID13), DT-2 leverages this technological interest to foster deeper civic engagement. It uses technology as a catalyst to attract and involve citizens who might otherwise remain disengaged from public issues (Table 6.3).

DT-3 contributes to shifting the approach to e-participation by moving beyond merely soliciting feedback to actively engaging citizens and government officials in the design and implementation of e-participation initiatives. This practice is meant to support addressing existing barriers by adopting co-production, hence setting up environments where government officials and societal actors can interact. This

Table. 6.3 Alignment of "DT-3: Co-production" with e-participation barriers

| DT practice | ID | Barrier related | Needs | How DT can support e-participation |
|---|---|---|---|---|
| DT-3: Co-production | ID03 | Integration of e-participation into the actual government | Involving citizens and officials in design for effective integration | Promote playgrounds and settings for collaboration with government officials Demonstrate the relevance of e-participation initiatives to public administrations and government officials |
| | ID10 | Lack of citizens' willingness to produce content, reviews or feedbacks | Fostering active citizen involvement in content creation | Favour co-production settings and activities to involve citizens in content creation Enhance sense of ownership |
| | ID14 | Lack of transparency | Promoting transparency and active participation in platform design | Promote a transparent and participatory environment Clarify objects, processes, and outcomes of e-participation initiatives |
| | ID15 | Lurking behaviour | Encouraging more active engagement in e-participation platforms | Support creation of collaborative settings for knowledge exchange Foster a sense of community and ownership |

## 6.1 E-Participation Barriers Against DT Practices

setup, similar to experimental laboratories, not only allows for the direct involvement of citizens in the governance process but engages multiple relevant actors in the activities. This demonstrates to the different stakeholders, public administrators and technology providers included, the practical benefits and relevance of encouraging collaborative activities via e-participation. Additional support can be provided to tackle the issue of citizens' reluctance to produce content (ID10), with the establishment of settings that encourage co-creation of content, co-design and co-production of solutions. This practice helps include multiple perspectives, while cultivating a sense of ownership and responsibility among participants, emphasising the tangible impact of their contributions on decision-making processes and the broader public agenda. This practice is also related to the mitigation of lurking behaviours (ID15).

Lastly, addressing the lack of transparency (ID14), DT-3 promotes environments that are open, equitable, and participatory, where the processes and outcomes of e-participation are clearly communicated and made visible to all stakeholders (Table 6.4).

DT-4 leverages a dynamic, iterative approach to developing e-participation both in terms of initiatives and platforms. This practice fosters direct collaboration with multiple stakeholders, including citizens, technology providers, NGOs, associations,

Table. 6.4 Alignment of "DT-4: Experimentation and prototyping" with e-participation barriers

| DT practice | ID | Barrier related | Needs | How DT can support e-participation |
|---|---|---|---|---|
| DT-4: Experimentation and prototyping | ID01 | Digital illiteracy | Designing for users with varying digital skills; iteratively testing with users | Favour iterative testing to create more user-friendly designs. Inform the e-participation platforms and journeys with needs of users with low or absent digital illiteracy |
| | ID02 | Difficult internet access or IT equipment to participate | Designing accessible platforms for low-resource environments | Develop e-participation environments accessible for resource-constrained environments. Ensure platforms are viable and effective for all users |
| | ID04 | Lack of accessibility | Creating user-friendly and disability-accessible platforms | Encourage inclusivity by design. Consider the needs of users with diverse abilities |
| | ID11 | Privacy issues | Testing secure and privacy-compliant e-participation platforms | Adopt iterative testing with the users to experimenting with privacy controls and data security measures. Ensure platforms reliability and accountability to address privacy concerns |

and public officials, engaged in experimenting with prototypes. Such experimentation takes place in real but controlled environments that serve as safer spaces for trialling solutions, thus minimising risks before broader implementations. This practice becomes particularly relevant in low-resource settings or those with limited technology, where the trial of novel approaches allows for feasibility and effectiveness evaluation before scaling.

DT-4 helps address the challenge of digital illiteracy (ID01) by allowing for the design of platforms that are intuitive and easy to use. Testing with users with varying levels of digital skills allows designers to refine and adapt the platforms to meet the diverse needs of the users effectively. As such, DT-4 supports fine-tuning interfaces and functionalities to ensure they meet the diverse digital skills of users (ID01), enhancing accessibility for all, including those with disabilities (ID04).

While DT-4 is adept at refining and optimising e-participation platforms for better user experience, limited support can be given to tackle issues related to users who face difficulties in terms of internet access or inadequate IT equipment (ID02). However, DT-4 can support the design of solutions that adapt across various environments, also those with low-resource and low-end technology. As such, while DT can help develop alternative solutions, it alone cannot resolve fundamental challenges related to access, infrastructure, or IT equipment deficiencies that hinder e-participation. Finally, for addressing privacy concerns (ID11), this DT practice can encourage testing e-participation security measures and privacy controls throughout the design process. Specifically, it can support experimentation of privacy-by-design principles which prioritise user privacy from the outset, increasing citizen's trust regarding the handling and protection of their data. Iterative testing with users helps in identifying and resolving potential security vulnerabilities early in the development phase, thereby enhancing trustworthy data handling (Table 6.5).

DT-5 concerns the transformative influence of DT in reshaping the institutional frameworks and processes within public administrations to foster more open, transparent, and citizen-responsive governance models. This practice draws attention to the role of knowledge transfer and capacity building, ensuring that the insights gained from various e-participation initiatives and experimentations are retained and put in place to drive continuous improvement and reflexivity within governmental entities. By advocating for a culture that values transparency and responsiveness (ID07), DT-5 can indeed encourage the adoption of more open practices that can build or strengthen trust among citizens, particularly in contexts with prevalent scepticism towards e-participation practices. This approach entails a shift towards governance structures where citizen feedback and engagement are seen as central elements of the policymaking and decision-making process, ensuring that decisions are visibly aligned with public interests and needs (ID09).

From a different perspective, DT-5 can contribute to the challenge of integrating technology into public engagement processes (ID13) by bridging the gap between enthusiastic interest for technological advances and their practical, meaningful application for hearing citizen voices. This practice not only leverages possible desires to experiment with new or trendy technologies, but also ensures that their inclusion is beneficial and impactful to both citizens and the public sector.

6.2 A Focus on DT Practices for Public Sector Organisations

**Table. 6.5** Alignment of "DT-5: Changing organisational culture" with e-participation barriers

| DT practice | ID | Barrier related | Needs | How DT can support e-participation |
|---|---|---|---|---|
| DT-5: Changing organisational culture | ID07 | Low levels of confidence in politicians | Developing a culture of transparency and responsiveness | Engage governmental officials to make their practices more transparent and responsive to citizens |
| | ID09 | Lack of alignment between the topics being discussed and the daily issues and priorities of the citizen | Shifting focus to address issues relevant to citizens | Advocate for alignment of e-participation initiatives with citizen-centric issues Strengthen the link between public concerns and governmental governmental decisions |
| | ID13 | Lack of interest in public affairs although enthusiasm for new technology | Bridging the gap between tech enthusiasm and civic engagement | Bridge the gap between technological enthusiasm and how technology is used for effective engagement Inform technology adoption based on citizens and organisational needs Foster an organisational mindset that favours effective and focused public engagement |

## 6.2 A Focus on DT Practices for Public Sector Organisations

The implications of our findings extend beyond theoretical constructs, offering practical pathways for public organisations to implement e-participation more effectively.

Public organisations can benefit by adopting co-design processes (**DT-3: Co-production**) that actively engage citizens and officials. Collaborative workshops and co-creation sessions can be put in place to gather different perspectives, leading to practical and relevant outcomes. This means bringing together citizens, government officials, and other stakeholders in structured yet creative environments which favour interactions among a diverse array of stakeholders. As a result, a wide range of perspectives can feed into the decision-making process, leading to outcomes that are more inclusive and practically applicable to varied community needs. By embedding co-design and co-production practices, public organisations can transform traditional engagement mechanisms into dynamic, digitally enhanced settings where citizen input is not only solicited but is foundational to the development process.

Public organisations can implement strategies to motivate passive users to become active contributors in e-participation initiatives (**DT-2: Publics formation**), fostering the inclusion of diverse viewpoints and supporting constructive discourse. Publics formation refers to the process of identifying, engaging, and mobilising diverse groups of people who are affected by or interested in specific public issues. Within the e-participation discourse, public formations means to go beyond the engagement of the most vocal or readily accessible citizens for actively involving in the process of policy-making, service design, and decision-making a wider variety of citizens. This concept is rooted in the idea that different communities may have unique needs and perspectives that should be considered to make governance truly democratic and effective. Encouraging expert publics to participate actively enhances inclusivity and relevance, creating a community-driven environment that encourages active participation and collaboration. By employing targeted approaches that address the barriers to participation—whether they be technological, cultural, or psychological—DT helps in fostering an inclusive environment where every citizen feels empowered to contribute.

By implementing iterative testing and prototyping (**DT-4: Experimentation and prototyping**), public sector organisations can collaborate with technical players and citizens to inform the creation of more user-friendly e-participation platforms based on real-world usage and feedback. In designing interfaces and processes, public administrations should pay attention to catering to diverse user groups, including those with varying levels of digital literacy. Embracing inclusive design principles guarantees that e-participation platforms are accessible to all citizens, including those with disabilities. In this sense, public organisations can leverage this aspect of DT to trial new features or interfaces in limited settings before wider deployment, reducing the risks associated with full-scale implementation and increasing the likelihood of acceptance and satisfaction among end-users.

To ensure that e-participation initiatives closely align with what truly matters to the public, informed by DT practices, public organisations should invest in a deep understanding of citizens' needs and priorities (**DT-1: Meaning creation and sense-making**). In e-participation practices and platforms, strategies should be put in place to enhance transparency and communication between politicians/governments and citizens, prioritising accountability and openness to citizens' input, while keeping the public informed about how the outputs of deliberations are going to be considered. To address citizens' concerns about privacy, privacy measures and data protection policies should be clearly communicated. Building trust and confidence among users requires ensuring transparency in data handling and security.

Encouraging a shift from a technology-driven to a design-driven approach in e-participation (**DT-5: Changing organisational culture**) promotes more desirable innovation, adaptability, and also user-centricity in decision-making processes. Strategically investing time and resources in capacity building and knowledge transfer is key for supporting a culture of continuous improvement that is aware and responsive to citizens' needs and evolving expectations. This shift necessitates not only the adoption of new tools and practices but also a reorientation of values and goals towards greater inclusivity and responsiveness.

By adopting such recommendations, public organisations can create a more effective and transparent e-participation ecosystem able to tackle the needs and expectations of citizens, ultimately leading to better digital public services and governance mechanisms. However, several issues may prevent public administration from adopting DT practices. Relevant ones may point at resource constraints, resistance to change within bureaucratic structures, and the need for extensive capacity building and training. Integrating DT in e-participation does not simply constitute an opportunity for improving bottom-up processes but could also be regarded as a risk of disruption of established procedures. Indeed, it presents several implications for the traditional top-down approach adopted by governments. This transformation challenges established cultures, potentially implying a major shift in the organisational and political culture of public institutions. Another critical point concerns the need to develop specific skills in facilitation and negotiation for public officials.

When viewed through the lens of organisational culture, governments that are not accustomed nor prone to experimentation tend to exhibit highest levels of resistance to embed e-participation into their practices. Such resistance primarily comes from a lack of understanding of the benefits and strengths, often combined with concerns about the potential effort involved in its implementation. To facilitate pathways for citizens to influence decision-making, changing organisational structures and procedures is also key. Failure to address this structural aspect can act as a significant obstacle, impeding the effective adoption and implementation of e-participation.

Furthermore, experts and decision-makers concur that achieving effectiveness in e-participation requires going beyond simple information dissemination or basic consultation approaches, preferring more proactive strategies. However, potential impediments might come from the side of citizens themselves. They feature varying levels of knowledge, resources, availability of time, willingness to participate, and levels of digital literacy. To mitigate potential disparities and inequalities stemming from these diversities, proactive measures should be adopted, ensuring that e-participation initiatives are inclusive, accessible, and truly representative of the broader population.

**Funding** Some of the reasoning presented in this work derive from knowledge and insights from the project "AI4GOV, Artificial Intelligence for Public Services", Action No. 2020-EU-IA-0064, co-financed by the EU CEF Telecom (No. INEA/CEF/ICT/A2020/2265375) [ai4gov-hub.eu; ai4gov-master.eu]. The opinions expressed herewith are solely of the authors and do not necessarily reflect the point of view of any EU institution.

# Reference

Oliveira C, Garcia ACB (2019) Citizens' electronic participation: as systematic review of their challenges and how to overcome them. Int J Web Based Communities 15(2):123–150. https://doi.org/10.1504/IJWBC.2019.101042

**Open Access** This chapter is licensed under the terms of the Creative Commons Attribution 4.0 International License (http://creativecommons.org/licenses/by/4.0/), which permits use, sharing, adaptation, distribution and reproduction in any medium or format, as long as you give appropriate credit to the original author(s) and the source, provide a link to the Creative Commons license and indicate if changes were made.

The images or other third party material in this chapter are included in the chapter's Creative Commons license, unless indicated otherwise in a credit line to the material. If material is not included in the chapter's Creative Commons license and your intended use is not permitted by statutory regulation or exceeds the permitted use, you will need to obtain permission directly from the copyright holder.

# Chapter 7
# Future Research Directions

**Abstract** This chapter explores areas for future research that extend beyond the scope of the current investigation, looking at the role of DT as a transformative approach for enhancing e-participation. Ultimately, it summarises how the work contributes to the current discourse.

**Keywords** E-Participation · Design thinking · Operational challenges · Future research

In light of the discourse so far presented, the implications and significance of our findings are specifically discussed to explore how DT principles and practices can address identified barriers to e-participation in digital public services. This work originated from challenges observed in e-participation literature, pointing out the difficulties in addressing user expectations. These barriers underline the need for targeted strategies to enhance effective and informed citizen engagement in e-participation, with DT offering key insights into addressing current issues and supporting public organisations in overcoming existing barriers.

## 7.1 Future DT-Related Research Areas

This chapter specifically explores **areas for future research** that extend beyond the scope of the current investigation. These span from investigating the long-term effects of DT implementation in public organisations, exploring additional DT practices that may strengthen and enhance e-participation, the conduction of case study analysis to assess the real-world impact of DT, and analysis on how to mitigate selection and technical biases which may reinforce the presence of echo chambers, further polarising the discourse and marginalising non-dominant voices.

Such research directions are explored in the following paragraphs.

## 7.1.1 Assessing DT Effectiveness and Impact on e-participation

The analysis conducted throughout this book underscores the relevance of further studies aimed at establishing a coherent framework to assess the effectiveness and impact of DT practices in e-participation. This framework should offer validated theoretical models and practical tools for monitoring and measuring the impact of DT adoption in various dimensions of e-participation. The importance of such a framework has been recognised for some time. In 2008, Macintosh and Whyte (2008) proposed an evaluation framework aimed at understanding e-participation applications and learning from these experiences. Even then, they noted the potential benefits of further developing their framework. This need has become increasingly urgent over time due to changes triggered by technological advancements and participatory habits. The ongoing need to develop a comprehensive set of theoretical and practical instruments that enable inclusive engagement highlights a significant gap. There is a clear demand for integrated fieldwork and methodologies that assess e-participation's social acceptance, incorporating diverse metrics such as user satisfaction, engagement levels, and policy impact. This area remains ripe for further investigation.

This book contributes to the ongoing discourse on assessing e-participation by introducing additional dimensions that enrich the discourse from a conceptual perspective. By integrating DT principles, it highlights the need for theoretical and practical instruments for measuring the efficacy of these practices in real-world settings. This approach encourages the consideration of integrating quantitative and qualitative metrics such as the depth of user involvement, the inclusiveness of participation processes, and the transformative impact of these initiatives on public trust and policy development.

## 7.1.2 Investigating the Impact of DT Implementation in Public Organisations

The implementation of DT in public organisations entails more than its timely application; it requires comprehensive and long-term institutionalisation. This process embeds DT deeply into both the structural and cultural frameworks of public governance, transforming it from a sporadic or project-based initiative into a sustained, routine activity within public administration (McGann et al. 2018). Structurally, institutionalisation involves integrating DT into the formal infrastructure and procedures of public institutions. However, to transcend imposition and permeate the cognitive and behavioural layers of the organisation, aligning the values, norms, and behaviours of public officials with DT principles, a cultural shift is essential (Beckman and Barry 2007). Achieving this cultural acceptance becomes strategic to frame DT as a valued and deeply ingrained approach that enhances responsiveness and desirability.

Specific research should focus on the sustained effort and consequences of implementing DT principles and practices in public organisations and its effects on supporting e-participation integration, over an extended period. A longitudinal analysis might also shed light on the persistence of improvements in citizen engagement and the evolution of services and policies due to the adoption of DT practices, and to what extent such implementation requires the upskilling or even development of new expertise within organisations running e-participation initiatives.

To bridge this gap between theoretical frameworks and practical outcomes, future research should focus on empirical case studies and explore public organisations that have implemented DT principles and practices in their e-participation initiatives. Such case studies can provide practical insights and concrete evidence on the transformative potential derived from embedding DT in designing e-participation practices and their influence on digital public services. In these terms, case studies can help document the application, challenges, and outcomes of DT-driven e-participation practices and initiatives, observing and measuring, for instance, tangible results such as increased citizen engagement and representation of multiple voices, service quality improvements, and policy efficacy. Additionally, attention should be posed on exploring the scalability of such initiatives and their adaptability across different governance contexts.

### 7.1.3 Tailoring DT Approaches to Context-Specific Barriers and Regulation Frameworks

Following the discourse on context-specificity, while this work has outlined a theoretical framework for leveraging DT principles and practices to enhance e-participation, the application and operationalization of DT requires to be finely tuned to meet the unique challenges, needs, and opportunities within specific e-governance contexts. It follows that DT contribution in enhancing e-participation cannot be assumed to be universal due to the significant influence of a variety of contextual factors. These include cultural specificities, regulatory frameworks, technological infrastructure, and political conditions, each of which can deeply impact how DT methodologies can be applied and how successful they can be in different settings.

As previously mentioned, a "one size fits all" approach is not only inappropriate but also undesirable when exploring e-participation, across diverse (e-)governance contexts. Each setting presents unique cultural dynamics that makes what works in one cultural setting ineffective in another due to differing social norms, values, and conditions (Åström et al. 2012; Müller and Skau 2015; Panopoulou et al. 2014). For instance, participatory techniques encouraging open confrontation and debate may be well-received in cultures with a tradition of direct and open debate, hence resonating well with the habits of the loci, but less so in contexts where indirect communication are more rooted and established. Similarly, regulatory frameworks vary widely, with some governments offering more flexibility and openness to innovative citizen engagement methods than others. The technological landscape also plays a crucial role. Regions with robust digital infrastructures can support more sophisticated and articulated e-participation applications, while those with limited technological access require adaptations to simpler, more accessible tools. Ultimately, also political conditions further affect e-participation. In politically stable environments, there might be more predisposition for long-term planning and experimentation of e-participation initiatives. In contrast, regions experiencing stronger resistance to new governance methods might face certain barriers to the adoption and effectiveness of these innovations.

DT can act as an agent of change within different settings. In more rigid or outdated regulatory frameworks, it can support deriving the needs on which to build innovative approaches through small-scale pilot projects. In such contexts, DT can provide evidence and trust, and build the case for more substantial reforms. This method of "change by doing" can gradually shift cultural, political, and regulatory environments towards more open and flexible governance structures. In more progressive settings that are open to digital transformation, DT can accelerate and enhance the integration of new e-participation technologies and methodologies. By facilitating collaboration between technology experts, government officials, and citizens, DT can be applied to push the boundaries of what is possible, encouraging the exploration of cutting-edge technologies and practices. Furthermore, DT's systemic and inclusive approach can help avoid that the integration of new technologies exacerbate existing inequalities or create new divides.

Recognising the role of diverse contextual factors in affecting citizen engagement and the efficacy of public service delivery, it becomes evident how specific research should focus on customising and tailoring DT practices to the distinct circumstances found across different e-governance environments. This involves not merely applying DT as a standardised model but adapting its methodologies to align with the local conditions—be they cultural, technological, or political. Specific research could explore the provision of actionable insights that significantly enhance the practicality and impact of citizen engagement initiatives.

Limited research has so far explored how to tailor approaches that help overcome barriers inherent in diverse administrative and cultural landscapes, facilitating more effective and sustainable citizen engagement strategies. This direction would encourage a more granular exploration of how DT can contribute to addressing specific governance challenges, ultimately leading to more robust and adaptive e-participation frameworks that are better aligned with the needs and expectations of various communities.

### 7.1.4 *Exploring Additional DT Methods and Techniques*

While the current work identifies specific DT practices that can enhance e-participation, there might be other DT methods and techniques that may also hold significant potential for enriching e-participation but not explored within the scope of this work. Future research could build on this foundational knowledge by delving deeper into existing DT toolboxes, exploring a broader array of methods and techniques. This exploration would uncover additional practices that could further streamline and improve e-participation processes. Beyond merely cataloguing a repertoire of DT tools, the research could systematically explore how each method enhances facets of e-participation. Such an inquiry would not only validate and possibly extend the practices already discussed but also identify innovative and more desirable ways to engage citizens and public officials more effectively. Potential methods could include advanced prototyping tools, deeper user research methodologies, or novel ideation techniques that foster more dynamic and inclusive participation. By operationalising these diverse DT methods, future studies may offer additional insights into how DT can be integrated into public engagement strategies, ensuring that the technological solutions align seamlessly with user needs and governance objectives.

## 7.2 Future Research Areas, Beyond DT

The paragraph above specifically explores DT-related areas for future research that extend beyond the scope of the current investigation. Next, the discussion shifts to identify additional future research areas that move beyond the DT confines, broadening the horizon for further inquiry in the field of e-participation.

### 7.2.1 Examining Appropriateness of e-participation

The existing literature underscores a noted gap regarding the appropriateness of e-participation in varying situations. While most studies have focused on the degree of engagement, they often overlook the critical aspect of how suitable e-participation is within specific social, cultural, or regulatory frameworks. The effectiveness of e-participation requires moving beyond mere information dissemination and routine consultations, towards proactive strategies that involve experts and decision-makers, tailored to resonate with societal, cultural, and regulatory norms.

Social capital factors like trust in government, community commitment, and a sense of community ownership significantly influence citizen engagement in e-participation (Van Dyne and Pierce 2004), far more than technological factors such as perceived usefulness and ease of use (Choi and Song 2020). Choi and Song's study (2020) highlights the direct correlation between higher levels of trust in government and strong community and the extent to which citizens are more likely to engage in e-participation. E-participation should, therefore, be designed to resonate with these social dynamics, potentially by facilitating more transparent interactions between citizens and government (Alharbi et al. 2016; Lee and Kim 2018). Future studies could explore the relationship between the effectiveness of e-participation initiatives and the social fabric of the community rather than just the technological infrastructure in explaining citizen's participation.

It could be valuable to explore how e-participation can be tailored to meet the unique challenges arising from different communities, ensuring cultural congruence and increased citizen engagement. Current research poses attention to the relevance of localising e-participation efforts to reflect the specific cultural and social makeup of the community, which can increase participation rates by making initiatives more relevant to the everyday lives of citizens (Oni et al. 2017). In light of this, specific attention could be posed to adopt design-driven and user-centred approaches to support deeper understanding and integration of the diverse, multi-level needs of a community, ensuring that the design of e-participation platforms not only addresses technological aspects but also aligns closely with the social, cultural, and behavioural contexts of the users.

Moreover, the relevance of e-participation also hinges on community commitment and the sense of ownership among citizens. Ideally, this sense of ownership can motivate citizens to use e-participation tools as a means of contributing to community development. Future studies should explore how e-participation can be effectively tailored to meet the unique challenges arising from different communities, ensuring cultural congruence. This approach requires a nuanced understanding of how various factors, including local governance structures, societal norms, and technological access, impact the effectiveness of e-participation initiatives. By focusing on the contextual suitability of e-participation, research can pave the way for more sophisticated and inclusive digital governance strategies that are directly aligned with the needs and expectations of diverse populations.

### 7.2.2 Exploring Generative AI Potential

Generative AI (GenAI) presents untapped potential for enhancing e-participation supporting both its practices and the platform usage. GenAI's capability to generate natural language outputs and visual content from textual descriptions offers novel ways to facilitate decision-making processes and foster more inclusive, productive participation in deliberative processes (von Brackel-Schmidt et al. 2024). Although GenAI has made significant strides, it has yet to be integrated in the e-participation domain. It holds particular promise for deliberative democracy, as it can help address barriers to participation that arise when specific skills are needed to effectively contribute to the process. These barriers often manifest as disparities in participants' ability to use digital tools, produce relevant texts, or create appropriate visual representations of ideas, prototypes, and visions (Tappert et al. 2024). In the domain of GenAI, models like GPT can produce outputs that closely resemble human responses to prompts typically presented in natural language interfaces. This capability not only enriches participant perspectives by offering diverse viewpoints but also aids in envisioning future scenarios and interpreting data.

7.2 Future Research Areas, Beyond DT

This potential is being currently explored through direct experimentation, such as the work by von Brackel-Schmidt and colleagues (2024). The researchers present a case involving 64 participants from multiple backgrounds tasked with collaboratively envisioning the future of The Hamburg metropolitan city in 2040. This case demonstrates that participants, irrespective of their backgrounds, could rapidly visualise their concepts for the city's future without requiring specific artistic or technical skills. They designed prompts using ChatGPT, then visualised through DALL-E 2, showing a practical application of GenAI chaining in urban planning. The accessibility and intuitive nature of GenAI's natural language interfaces indeed offer a viable and user-friendly solution to bridging the skill gap among participants, thus mitigating disparities and promoting more inclusive participation (Jiang et al. 2022). While the integration of GenAI into e-participation frameworks heralds significant potential advancements, it concurrently presents challenges that require consideration. The main challenge concerns the capacity to harness the full spectrum of GenAI's capabilities while balancing the possible unintended consequences detrimental to the integrity of participatory processes (Belanche et al. 2024; Sætra 2023). For instance, GenAI's ability to fabricate persuasive yet factually inaccurate content represents a relevant risk, particularly in the manipulation of deliberative discourse and possible dissemination of misleading information or fake news. Such risks are profoundly pertinent to the deliberative context, where the truthfulness, accuracy, and quality of information are of prime importance.

Ongoing research lines are already exploring GenAI to produce analytics and reports that support both online and in-person deliberation, or summarise their outcomes, enhancing real-time moderation and ensuring outputs are inclusive, transparent, and foster trust. However, a critical aspect that requires thorough exploration is maintaining a "human in the loop" approach. This approach ensures that human oversight is integrated into the GenAI workflows, providing a check against the potential biases and errors that AI systems might propagate.

To operationalise this, research should explore the development of systems where GenAI outputs are not only automatically generated but also reviewed and supervised by human moderators, thus refining and validating AI-generated contents before being used in decision-making processes or disseminated among participants. Furthermore, implementing feedback mechanisms would nurture continuous and real-time input from users, enhancing the training of the GenAI models. Models would largely benefit from such mechanisms, since they would be exposed to a diverse array of human interactions, new information, or changing dynamics in deliberative discussions.

### 7.2.3 Preventing Biases and the Creation of Echo Chambers

In e-participation, biases can emerge in two principal forms: selection bias and technical bias, each contributing significantly to the creation of echo chambers (Ross Arguedas et al. 2022) that skew discussions and exacerbate polarisation.

As previously introduced, selection bias occurs when the demographics participating in e-participation platforms are not representative of the wider community, often due to barriers such as digital literacy, access to technology, or simply varying levels of interest and motivation to engage. As such, selection bias poses a significant challenge in public deliberation processes, particularly where participation is influenced by physical accessibility or the digital divide, thus emerging as a key issue in need of exploration. As traditional in-person participation often excludes large segments of the population due to logistical constraints, e-participation also comes with barriers to participation, prompting the need of exploring how to enhance scalability and reach while mitigating exclusion means and inadvertent biassed outcomes. The dilemma is that larger, unfiltered participant groups often do not equate to balanced representation (Hartz-Karp and Sullivan 2014). Essentially, the ease of scaling up participation through digital means can attract participants who are already digitally savvy or particularly motivated by the topic, which may not provide a balanced view of the wider community's opinions. Furthermore, disadvantaged groups may prefer traditional representative democracy over deliberative approaches, which can amplify the voices of privileged segments, reinforcing existing biases in mini-publics (Talukder and Pilet 2021; Escobar and Elstub 2017). The challenge lies therefore in avoiding capturing the most vocal or most connected users but truly representing the diverse spectrum of society. Experimentation could explore strategies to engage diverse population segments, as demonstrated by the #MyFrance2022 initiative, which successfully broadened participation through targeted outreach and awareness campaigns.

Technical bias, on the other hand, arises from the algorithms, training data, and data processing techniques employed by digital platforms (Friedman and Nissenbaum 1996; Mittelstadt et al. 2016). These algorithms, often designed to enhance user engagement, can inadvertently prioritise and amplify certain types of interactions and information. For instance, summarisation algorithms can oversimplify complex discussions, potentially filtering out nuanced or minority opinions in favour of more dominant voices. Predictive algorithms, intended to anticipate user preferences and tailor content accordingly, can also contribute to this issue by creating feedback loops that reinforce users' existing beliefs. Furthermore, algorithms feeding users content based on past engagement can reinforce existing beliefs and viewpoints, limiting exposure to differing opinions and fostering environments where like-minded individuals reinforce each other's views.

Selection biases in participants and technical biases in developing e-participation platforms can inadvertently reinforce echo chambers, where similar viewpoints are amplified (confirmation bias and groupthink), and dissenting voices are marginalised or excluded. To mitigate these risks, future research should explore strategies for designing more inclusive algorithms that actively counteract biases by ensuring that they are trained on diverse data sets. This includes not only demographic diversity but also diversity in thought and opinion. Moreover, there should be an emphasis on transparency in how these algorithms operate and how they are applied within e-participation platforms, allowing users to understand and possibly challenge the way information is being curated and presented. Such approaches would help to break down echo chambers and foster a more genuinely representative and democratic e-participation environment.

Future research could vet into devising methodologies to effectively counteract both selection and technical biases from the initial stages of e-participation platform development, avoiding the formation of echo chambers. To move beyond theoretical discussions, the experimentation should concern actionable plans for operationalising concepts of better inclusion by design, also deriving practical recommendations for meaningful integration of diverse groups. The direction for future research should therefore consider better exploring the echo chambers phenomenon in e-participation and current deliberative processes, with the aim of actively designing strategies for breaking or preventing these cycles.

### 7.2.4 Exploring Asynchronous and Hybrid Interactions

This last paragraph transitions into a domain primarily rooted in design exploration rather than research directions. It examines the need to explore ways for blending traditional face-to-face deliberation methods with digital tools, thereby preserving the immediacy and depth of conventional methods. The emphasis here is on the proactive design and testing of innovative methods and models with the potential to transform the current landscape of e-participation.

Conventional deliberation typically occurs in face-to-face meetings, characterised by a structured agenda and short, frequent interactions among participants. However, such meetings inherently limit participant numbers, excluding those who cannot travel or commit to specific times, often across diverse geographical areas. This limitation restricts participation, especially for those unable to travel or align with the set schedule. In contrast, online deliberation leverages digital tools to transcend physical constraints, offering a broader, less resource-intensive participation opportunity, under the condition of having digital means to access it. Furthermore, digital settings often provide a longer timeframe for deliberation with a process composed of multiple phases, which can accommodate participants across different time zones and personal schedules. This structure is particularly advantageous for managing the high volume of inputs typical in online forums, ensuring that discussions are comprehensive and that more individuals have the opportunity to contribute meaningfully and at their convenience.

Digital tools integral to online deliberation—such as forums for commenting, voting mechanisms, and polls—support a range of interactive activities. While these tools can operate in real-time, digital deliberation predominantly unfolds asynchronously, allowing participants time for thoughtful reflection between contributions. This extended period can deepen discourse quality, though it may reduce the immediacy and dynamic interaction of face-to-face discussions. Spacing out interactions and decision-making steps fosters a thorough examination of topics, but this extended timeline might diminish the spontaneity found in live debates. Thus, strategic use of digital tools not only expands participation but also promotes a more deliberate, reflective engagement, potentially leading to more considered outcomes. Despite these advantages, e-participation is not seen as fully comparable to on-site participation by several scholars (Borchers et al. 2024; Maaroufi et al. 2021; Velhinho and Almeida 2023). Current e-participation management typically organises synchronous communication across several weeks, aiming to mitigate interaction challenges due to delayed responses (Schrammeijer et al. 2022). However, this can lead to contributions that are often insufficient and vague (Roman and Fellnhofer 2022).

Although digital tools are primarily designed for online deliberation, significant potential exists to enhance in-person assemblies and discussions, fostering hybrid forms of participation. Currently, little attention is drawn on integrating digital tools into traditional in-person deliberation processes. Yet, as the vTaiwan case illustrates, in-person interactions remain crucial and can be substantially enriched by digital enhancements. Organisers of deliberative activities could benefit from experimenting with methodologies that seamlessly blend virtual and in-person deliberations, tailoring their integration to different participation phases to maximise outcomes. A hybrid approach could augment the benefits of face-to-face interactions—such as immediate feedback, nuanced communication, and stronger relational connections—with the efficiency and reach of digital tools. To support such hybrid deliberations, digital platforms should be equipped with functionalities that facilitate real-time interaction but also robust data analysis, including features like live summaries, clustering, visualisations, and analytics, providing immediate insights during meetings and aiding more informed, dynamic discussions.

Building on the insights presented, future research should delve into how the DT approach to iterative design and experimentation can pioneer new e-participation models which blend or integrate asynchronous and hybrid interactions. The field is in need of adaptable e-participation frameworks that not only blend the immediacy of face-to-face engagement with the broad accessibility of online platforms but also include by-design the tailoring of integrations to the unique cultural, social, and technological contexts of different communities. These models should be robust and versatile enough to address specific local needs while providing generalizable insights that can inform broader e-participation strategies. Such exploratory research will be crucial in identifying best practices for designing participation processes that are both inclusive and effective, paving the way for more dynamic and responsive democratic engagements. Additional studies should be conducted to vet into the benefits and mostly the challenges and obstacles hindering such models, being aware and considerate of the high context-dependency of participatory practices.

This exploration could rely on DT principles and practices, and engage a diverse array of stakeholders in co-designing alternative methodologies that harness both the immediacy of in-person activities and the expansive reach of online interactions. These frameworks should be designed as adaptable templates that organisations can customise based on specific needs and contexts before implementation.

## 7.3 Limits of the Study

While this work offers promising insights for addressing current challenges, it also acknowledges some **limitations**. In particular, the scope of the work primarily focuses on the alignment between e-participation barriers and DT practices. This focus leaves out of the current scope a closer and contextual investigation of practical challenges that public organisations may face when operationalizing DT in e-participation. Exploring such limits more closely can significantly complement the results presented. Another limit regards the scale and context of this work. It mainly draws from a Western context, which may limit the generalisability and scalability of findings to other regions. It is therefore recognised that additional effort should regard the exploration of the applicability of DT principles in e-participation within **diverse global settings** to provide a more comprehensive understanding of its potential impact. In this regard, the effectiveness of DT principles and practices in e-participation can be contingent on multiple factors such as the political context, technological infrastructure, and the level of actual stakeholder engagement.

## 7.4 Conclusions

Overall, this work has addressed a specific set of challenges and barriers emerged from the scientific literature on e-participation, focusing predominantly from a citizen-centred perspective (Oliveira and Garcia 2019). It paves the way for future research that shifts the emphasis towards public administrations, contributing to the ongoing discourse on digital governance and public sector innovation. This study has stressed the meaningfulness of adopting a systemic and adaptive DT approach, tailored to the unique complexities and specificities that characterise the contemporary public sector alongside the evolving needs of citizens and communities.

Efforts have been specifically directed towards bridging the theoretical foundations of how DT can enhance e-participation with its potential practical applications, informing the development and implementation of novel or revised practices and tools. The result is a comprehensive hybrid framework for public organisations that outlines a clear, actionable pathway for integrating DT into public sector strategies to make e-participation more effective, inclusive, and deliberative. This orientation is aimed at making the insights and methods discussed not only conceptually robust but also directly applicable in real-world settings, empowering public organisations to enact meaningful and sustainable changes in the way they engage with citizens.

Ultimately, a necessary clarification to be made regards the points of view adopted so far, which portrays DT and the broader design approach not as a prescriptive approach. Rather than providing detailed guidelines or procedures on achieving desired outcomes, this book champions an exploratory and iterative approach that encourages flexibility and adaptability, allowing solutions to emerge organically from the process rather than being imposed from the outset. Thus, this book intends to serve as a dynamic scaffold, supporting multiple and multi-level stakeholders in navigating the many-sided challenges they face, providing them with the necessary knowledge to plan digital stakeholder engagement creatively and effectively, enhancing the overall quality of digitally-enhanced or boosted democratic participation.

This book provides a structured and comprehensive approach for public administrations and technology providers, facilitating the development and refinement of e-participation strategies and tools. For public administrations, it delineates a framework for embedding DT principles and practices to enhance public sector innovation, focusing on operative applications to improve the efficacy and inclusiveness of e-participation. For technology providers, the book serves as a guide to understanding and embedding the requirements of digital governance, aligning their offerings with the needs of the public sector, so that technological solutions not only meet technical demands of public engagement but support the more complex dynamics of digitally-enhanced democratic participation. Ultimately, this perspective shifts the emphasis from seeking predetermined solutions to fostering a culture of innovation and experimentation in conducive and participatory environments where multi-stakeholder engagement is central to nurture effective outcomes.

**Funding** Some of the reasoning presented in this work derive from knowledge and insights from the project "AI4GOV, Artificial Intelligence for Public Services", Action No. 2020-EU-IA-0064, co-financed by the EU CEF Telecom (No. INEA/CEF/ICT/A2020/2265375) [ai4gov-hub.eu; ai4gov-master.eu]. The opinions expressed herewith are solely of the authors and do not necessarily reflect the point of view of any EU institution.

# References

Alharbi A, Kang K, Hawryszkiewycz, I (2016) The influence of trust and subjective norms on citizens intentions to engage in E-participation on E-government Websites. https://arxiv.org/abs/1606.00746

Åström J, Karlsson M, Linde J, Pirannejad A (2012) Understanding the rise of e-participation in non-democracies: Domestic and international factors. Gov Inf Q 29(2):142–150. https://doi.org/10.1016/j.giq.2011.09.008

Beckman SL, Barry M (2007) Innovation as a learning process: embedding design thinking. Calif Manage Rev 50(1):25–56. https://doi.org/10.2307/41166415

Belanche D, Belk RW, Casaló LV, Flavián C (2024) The dark side of artificial intelligence in services. Serv Ind J 44(3–4):149–172. https://doi.org/10.1080/02642069.2024.2305451

Borchers M, Gierlich-Joas M, Tavanapour N, Bittner E (2024) Let citizens speak up: designing intelligent online participation for urban planning. In: Mandviwalla M, Söllner M, Tuunanen T (eds) Design science research for a resilient future. Springer Nature Switzerland, Cham, pp 18–32

Choi J-C, Song C (2020) Factors explaining why some citizens engage in E-participation, while others do not. Gov Inf Q 37(4):101524. https://doi.org/10.1016/j.giq.2020.101524

Escobar O, Elstub S (2017) Forms of mini-publics: an introduction to deliberative innovations in democratic practice. New Democracy Foundation. https://www.newdemocracy.com.au/research/research-notes/399-forms-of-mini-publics

# References

Friedman B, Nissenbaum H (1996) Bias in computer systems. ACM Trans Inf Syst 14(3):330–347. https://doi.org/10.1145/230538.230561

Hartz-Karp J, Sullivan B (2014) The unfulfilled promise of online deliberation. J Public Deliberation 10(1):1–5. https://doi.org/10.16997/jdd.191

Jiang E, Olson K, Toh E, Molina A, Donsbach A, Terry M, Cai CJ (2022) PromptMaker: Prompt-based Prototyping with Large & nbsp; Language & nbsp; Models. In: Extended abstracts of the 2022 CHI conference on human factors in computing systems. Association for Computing Machinery, New York, NY, USA. https://doi.org/10.1145/3491101.3503564

Lee J, Kim S (2018) Citizens' e-participation on agenda setting in local governance: do individual social capital and e-participation management matter? Public Manag Rev 20(6):873–895. https://doi.org/10.1080/14719037.2017.1340507

Maaroufi MM, Stour L, Agoumi A (2021) Contribution of digital collaboration and e-learning to the implementation of smart mobility in Morocco. In: Motahhir S, Bossoufi B (eds) Digital technologies and applications. Springer International Publishing, Cham, pp 609–619

Macintosh A, Whyte A (2008) Towards an evaluation framework for eParticipation. Transform GovMent: People, Process Policy 2(1):16–30. https://doi.org/10.1108/17506160810862928

McGann M, Blomkamp E, Lewis JM (2018) The rise of public sector innovation labs: Experiments in design thinking for policy. Policy Sci 51(3):249–267. https://doi.org/10.1007/s11077-018-9315-7

Mittelstadt BD, Allo P, Taddeo M, Wachter S, Floridi L (2016) The ethics of algorithms: mapping the debate. Big Data Soc 3(2):2053951716679679. https://doi.org/10.1177/2053951716679679

Müller SD, Skau SA (2015) Success factors influencing implementation of e-government at different stages of maturity: a literature review. Int J Electron GovAnce 7(2):136–170. https://doi.org/10.1504/IJEG.2015.069495

Oliveira C, Garcia ACB (2019) Citizens' electronic participation: A systematic review of their challenges and how to overcome them. Int J Web Based Communities 15(2):123–150. https://doi.org/10.1504/IJWBC.2019.101042

Oni AA, Oni S, Mbarika V, Ayo CK (2017) Empirical study of user acceptance of online political participation: integrating civic voluntarism model and theory of reasoned action. Gov Inf Q 34(2):317–328. https://doi.org/10.1016/j.giq.2017.02.003

Panopoulou E, Tambouris E, Tarabanis K (2014) Success factors in designing eParticipation initiatives. Inf Organ 24(4):195–213. https://doi.org/10.1016/j.infoandorg.2014.08.001

Roman M, Fellnhofer K (2022) Facilitating the participation of civil society in regional planning: implementing quadruple helix model in finnish regions. Land Use Policy 112:105864. https://doi.org/10.1016/j.landusepol.2021.105864

Ross Arguedas A, Robertson C, Fletcher R, Nielsen R (2022) Echo chambers, filter bubbles, and polarisation: a literature review. Reuters Institute for the Study of Journalism

Sætra HS (2023) Generative AI: Here to stay, but for good? Technol Soc 75:102372. https://doi.org/10.1016/j.techsoc.2023.102372

Schrammeijer EA, van Zanten BT, Davis J, Verburg PH (2022) The advantage of mobile technologies in crowdsourcing landscape preferences: Testing a mobile app to inform planning decisions. Urban for & Urban Green 73:127610. https://doi.org/10.1016/j.ufug.2022.127610

Talukder D, Pilet JB (2021) Public support for deliberative democracy. A specific look at the attitudes of citizens from disadvantaged groups. Innovation: Eur J Soc Sci Res 34(5):656–676. https://doi.org/10.1080/13511610.2021.1978284

Tappert S, Mehan A, Tuominen P, Varga Z (2024) Citizen participation, Digital agency, and urban development. Urban planning, vol 9 (2024). Citizen participation, digital agency, and urban development. https://doi.org/10.17645/up.7810

Van Dyne L, Pierce JL (2004) Psychological ownership and feelings of possession: three field studies predicting employee attitudes and organizational citizenship behavior. J Organ Behav 25(4):439–459. https://doi.org/10.1002/job.249

Velhinho A, Almeida P (2023) POLARISCOPE—A platform for the co-creation and visualization of collective memories. In: Marcus A, Rosenzweig E, Soares MM (eds) Design, user experience, and usability. Springer Nature Switzerland, Cham, pp 273–285

von Brackel-Schmidt C, Kučević E, Leible S, Simic D, Gücük GL, Schmidt FN (2024) Equipping participation formats with generative AI: a case study predicting the future of a metropolitan city in the year 2040. In: Nah FFH, Siau KL (eds) HCI in business, government and organizations). Springer Nature Switzerland, Cham, pp 270–285

**Open Access** This chapter is licensed under the terms of the Creative Commons Attribution 4.0 International License (http://creativecommons.org/licenses/by/4.0/), which permits use, sharing, adaptation, distribution and reproduction in any medium or format, as long as you give appropriate credit to the original author(s) and the source, provide a link to the Creative Commons license and indicate if changes were made.

The images or other third party material in this chapter are included in the chapter's Creative Commons license, unless indicated otherwise in a credit line to the material. If material is not included in the chapter's Creative Commons license and your intended use is not permitted by statutory regulation or exceeds the permitted use, you will need to obtain permission directly from the copyright holder.

# Annex

*Projects Contributing to the Work*

| Project extended title | Funding prog. and duration | Objectives | Contribution to the analysis |
|---|---|---|---|
| AI4GOV. Artificial Intelligence for Public Services | CEF Telecom, 2021–2024 | AI4Gov is a leading international ecosystem of research, training, and innovation opportunities aiming to use AI to improve public services, globally. The project designs and delivers a master programme to cover: (i) the management of AI-based public services, (ii) the use of AI in the functioning of public administration, and (iii) AI governance for the public sector and public service delivery in society. The result is the training of functional specialists in both AI and public services with a focus on AI governance and ethics for public services, both in a specific module and in all actions in practical contexts. The programme includes a special focus on AI governance and ethics from the perspective of public services | By focusing on functional specialists in AI, the project contributes foundational knowledge in e-participation and facilitates hands-on project work where theoretical concepts are tested and refined through diverse experimental cohorts, tackling varied topics. Moreover, AI4GOV's multidisciplinary framework has proven to be a fertile ground for garnering insights from multiple perspectives. Contributions from fields such as computer science, engineering, design, and political science enriched the discourse on e-participation, ensuring a holistic view that accommodates various stakeholder needs and insights. Exploring cutting-edge topics within its ecosystem, AI4GOV also acts indeed as a playground for enhancing knowledge. This setting enables continuous innovation and interaction among specialists, fostering a rich exchange of ideas and solutions that propel the discussion and implementation of AI-enhanced e-participation tools forward. In particular, it explores how forefront technology can meet usability and desirability in civic engagement |
| ORBIS. Augmenting participation, co-creation, trust and transparency in Deliberative Democracy at all scales | HEU, 2023–2026 | ORBIS addresses the disconnects between ambitious ideas and collective actions at a large socio-technical scale. It responds to the profound lack of dialogue between citizenship and policy making institutions by providing a theoretically sound and highly pragmatic socio-technical solution to enable the transition to a more inclusive, transparent and trustful Deliberative Democracy in Europe. ORBIS provides new ways to understand and facilitate the emergence of new participatory democracy models, together with the mechanisms to scale them up and consolidate them at institutional level | The project contributes to advance understanding regarding the effective adoption of digital tools to enhance public engagement. It also provides valuable insights into the challenges related to participation through an analysis of the deliberative democracy research landscape. Additionally, the project involves six pilot initiatives, offering essential requirements for enhancing participation and fostering deliberative democracy through the application of digital tools |

(continued)

(continued)

| Project extended title | Funding prog. and duration | Objectives | Contribution to the analysis |
|---|---|---|---|
| NEUROCLIMA. Developing and assessing novel educational user-centred actions towards scaling up behavioural change and climate resilience through AI-enhanced solutions | HEU; 2024–2027 | NEUROCLIMA is designed to establish a novel framework for supporting and sustaining systemic transformations and citizen engagement towards climate resilience. This project aims to create an AI-enhanced system that meaningfully connects policy makers, public institutions, and citizens, ensuring responsiveness to citizens' concerns, environmental changes, and policy updates. The project also seeks to empower citizens and decision-makers by capitalising on strategic leverage points and enhancing climate literacy, thus supporting informed participation in climate change adaptation | The project contributes by integrating reflections on advanced digital tools to enhance public engagement in environmental governance, aimed at improving the quality of dialogue between citizens and policymakers, making the decision-making process more inclusive and transparent. The project is also investigating usable and intuitive platforms for online dialogue that addresses current gaps in participatory democracy tools, which often lack support for structured and evidence-based reasoning. This will enhance the ability of these platforms to support meaningful and productive citizen participation in climate-related decision-making processes |
| NZC. Accelerating cities' transition to net zero emissions by 2030 | H2020, 2021–2025 | The EU-funded NetZeroCities project will support European cities in significantly reducing greenhouse gas emissions to achieve climate neutrality. The initiative supports the European Green Deal to realise a low-carbon, climate-resilient future through research and innovation. Bringing together 33 partners from 13 countries, the project will help cities overcome structural, institutional and cultural barriers in order to achieve climate neutrality by 2030. Specifically, NetZeroCities will develop a service-oriented platform, co-create solutions, and develop new and improve existing tools, resources and expertise | The project contributes by establishing effective citizen engagement methodologies tailored to local public administrations, including their use of digital tools. The project's interactions with over 100 cities have provided insights into the complexities and issues faced by public administrations when engaging citizens and stakeholders in the context of climate action |

(continued)

(continued)

| Project extended title | Funding prog. and duration | Objectives | Contribution to the analysis |
|---|---|---|---|
| GovTech Connect. Fostering Digitisation of Public Sector and Green Transition in Europe through the Use of an Innovative European GovTech Platform | DG CNECT, 2022–2024 | The GovTech platform is a pilot project that aims to support public administrations in the adoption of cost-effective and flexible digital solutions through the introduction of the GovTech ecosystem to the European public sector. It follows the platform model seen in GovTech labs around Europe, helping public administrations to work together and share solutions | This project significantly contributes to the understanding of the barriers encountered by public sectors in the adoption of Design Thinking (DT) principles and practices for service innovation and stakeholder engagement. Moreover, insights from interactions with startups developing GovTech solutions have revealed structural and cultural obstacles that public sectors confront |
| SISCODE. Society in Innovation and Science through CO-DEsign | H2020, 2018–2021 | The project aimed to understand co-creation as a bottom-up and design-driven phenomenon that is flourishing in Europe (in fab labs, living labs, social innovations, smart cities, communities and regions) to analyse favourable conditions that support its effective introduction, scalability and replication, and to use this knowledge to cross-fertilise RRI practices and policies. The project investigated the role and potential application of co-creation processes activated by design as a framework for responsible research and innovation, involving civil society in scientific and technological innovation, and in particular in the inclusion of society in the development of more inclusive policies desired by citizens, overcoming barriers and resistance to change | The project offers extensive knowledge and expertise in running co-creation processes to design innovative and desirable solutions, particularly within the context of informing policy-making. Drawing from extensive 18-month experimentation across ten pilots across Europe, it provides valuable insights into the successful implementation of co-design and co-production processes in innovative ecosystems of co-creation |

(continued)

(continued)

| Project extended title | Funding prog. and duration | Objectives | Contribution to the analysis |
|---|---|---|---|
| easyRights. Improved public services for successful migrant integration | H2020, 2020–2022 | Efforts to integrate immigrants at the local level are based on the need to provide them with good quality public services, reducing bureaucracy in order to promote the possibility of acting with more autonomy and to facilitate integration. To this end, EASYRIGHTS supports the co-creation of a system by different local actors that increases the quantity and quality of public services offered to immigrants. It deploys a platform envisaging the engagement of local stakeholders and to collect both online and offline services in four pilot cities. In addition, it supports immigrants to achieve knowledge and understanding for better and easier access to public services | The project provides valuable insights into the effective implementation of co-creation with public administrations, with a specific focus on improving access to public services—particularly for migrants. The knowledge gained extends to the design of innovative and desirable solutions, based on extensive experimentation conducted in four different pilot locations across the EU over nearly two years. During the piloting, end-users were constantly involved, from the early stages of context analysis and problem framing up to the testing and validation of the digital solutions |

**SPRINGER NATURE**

## GPSR Compliance

The European Union's (EU) General Product Safety Regulation (GPSR) is a set of rules that requires consumer products to be safe and our obligations to ensure this.

If you have any concerns about our products, you can contact us on ProductSafety@springernature.com

In case Publisher is established outside the EU, the EU authorized representative is:

Springer Nature Customer Service Center GmbH
Europaplatz 3
69115 Heidelberg, Germany

The manufacturer's authorised representative in the EU is Springer Nature Customer Service Centre GmbH, Europaplatz 3, 69115 Heidelberg, Germany. If you have any concerns regarding our products, please contact ProductSafety@springernature.com

Printed and bound by CPI Group (UK) Ltd, Croydon, CR0 4YY

26/03/2026

02078953-0014